IMAGES OF WALES

ABERGAVENNY PUBS

IMAGES OF WALES

ABERGAVENNY PUBS

FRANK OLDING

TEMPUS

This book is dedicated to Doug and Lou McArthur for their love of Abergavenny and its pubs!

First published 2005

Tempus Publishing Limited
The Mill, Brimscombe Port,
Stroud, Gloucestershire, GL5 2QG

British Library Cataloguing in Publication Data.
A catalogue record for this book is available from the British Library.

ISBN 0 7524 3576 0

Typesetting and origination by Tempus Publishing Limited
Printed in Great Britain

Contents

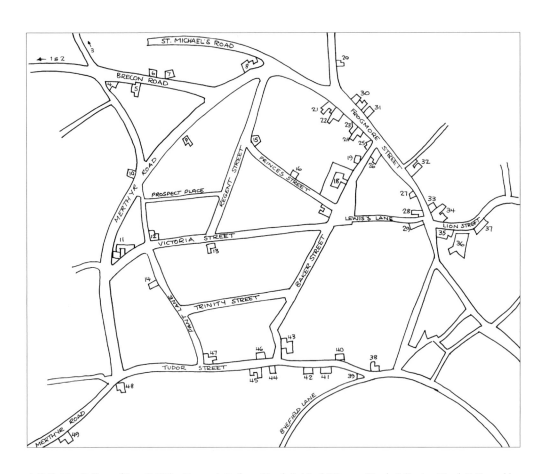

1-Belle Vue, 2-Cantref Inn, 3-Cider House, 4-Railway Hotel, 5-North Western Hotel, 6-Station Hotel, 7-Reynolds and Wase's Brewery, 8-Brecon Road Brewery, 9-No. 24, Merthyr Road, 10-Lamb Inn, 11-Somerset Arms Inn, 12-Mount Pleasant Inn, 13-Beaufort Arms, 14-Cock and Bottle, 15-Albert Inn, 16-Carpenter's Arms, 17-Grofield Inn, 18-Royal Victoria Brewery, 19-Carpenter's Arms, 20-Haulier's Arms, 21-Butcher's Arms, 22-George Inn, 23-Three Salmons, 24-George Hotel, 25-Bell Inn, 26-Britannia, 27-Griffin Inn, 28-King David Inn, 29-Lamb Inn, 30-Boot, 31-Old Herefordshire House, 32-White Horse Inn, 33-King William, 34-Golden Lion, 35-Green Dragon, 36-Ellis' Brewery, 37-William Morgan and Co. Brewery, 38-Albion Inn, 39-Tudor Arms, 40-Blue Bell Inn, 41-Tudor Inn, 42-No. 26, Tudor Street, 44-Milkman's Arms, 45-Cooper's Arms, 46-Old Cross Keys Inn, 47-Forester's Arms, 48-Beaufort Arms, 49-White Lion.

Sources

GENERAL SOURCES
The lists of publicans and owners are largely drawn from the Rate Books and the various trade directories that give detailed lists of businesses and traders in Abergavenny between the late eighteenth century and the 1920s. Reference copies of these directories can be consulted at Abergavenny Museum.

Originally, detailed references to the many hundreds of documents consulted in the preparation of this book were included in comprehensive notes. These have been omitted at the request of the publisher, but a properly annotated typescript has been deposited at Abergavenny Museum.

PRIMARY SOURCES
Abergavenny Museum
Abergavenny Poor Rate Book, 1839 (A.238-1984),1853 (A.76-1981) 1858-59 (A.299-1981)
Abergavenny Street and Water Rate Book, 1860 (AL/8-1981), 1868 (A.3219-0), 1873 (A.3218-0)
Petition to the Improvement Commissioners for a public recreation ground, 1876 (A.72-1981)
Petition to the Improvement Commissioners 'to have the Cattle Market Gate, next to Dr Smythe's House, opened on Market and Fair days for the convenience of taking in the Cattle, 1876 (A.71-1981)
Poll Book of Monmouthshire, 1847 (A.764-1978)
Price, William, 'Abergavenny at the Beginning of the Nineteenth Century', *Abergavenny Chronicle* (1880)
Register of Persons Entitled to Vote ... the County of Monmouth, 1880 (A.3232-0)
Wood's Map of Abergavenny, 1834

Gwent Record Office
Abergavenny Improvement Commissioners' Minutes (D.874.1-10)
Abergavenny Vestry Meeting Minute Book, 1787 (D.874.92)
Abergavenny Rate Books, 1840 (D.874.111), 1850 (D.874.112), June 1851 (D.874.113), July 1851 (D.874.115), 1856 (D.874.114), 1857 (D.874.116), 1864 (D.874.71), 1872 (D.874.72), 1914 (D.874.73), 1938 (D.874.75), 1939 (D.874.76)
Abergavenny Tithe Apportionment, 1843 (D.615)
Anon. (*c.* 1880) *Recollections of Abergavenny by an Octogenarian* (D.992.5, p6)

SECONDARY SOURCES
Bradney, J.A., 1906, *A History of Monmouthshire: The Hundred of Abergavenny*, Vol. I, Pt 2a (9 vols; repr. Academy Books, 1992)
Cox, N. and A., 1994, *The Tokens, Checks, Metallic Tickets, Passes and Tallies of Wales 1800-1993* (N. and A. Cox, Cardiff)

Davies, P.M, 1977, *The Works of the Abergavenny Improvement Commissioners 1794-1854* (unpublished University of Wales thesis)

Glover, Brian, 1993, *Prince of Ales: the History of Brewing in Wales* (Alan Sutton, Stroud)

PERSONAL MEMOIRS

Thanks to Mr M.O. Roberts, Mrs Kathleen Evans, Mr Tom Winter, Mrs Elsie May Hall and Mr Bill King.

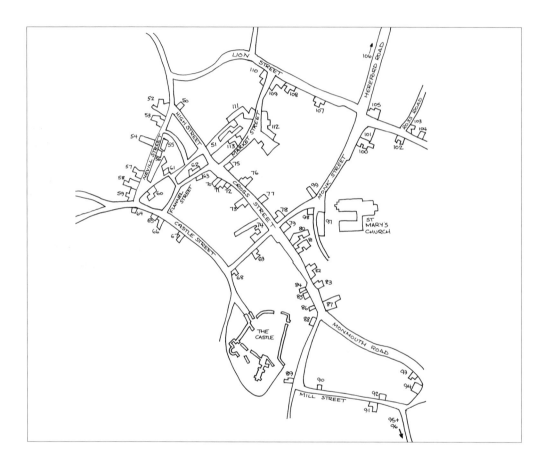

50-Guildhall Inn, 51-Greyhound Hotel, 52-Raven Hotel, 53-King's Head, 54-James Jones' Brewery, 55-Dragon's Head Inn, 56-Cow Inn, 57-Black-a-moor's Head, 58-Pye Bull, 59-King's Arms Inn, 60-Bull Inn, 61-Vine Tree, 62-Hen and Chickens, 63-Old Barley Mow, 64-White Swan, 65-Old Duke Inn, 66-New Duke Inn, 67-Beehive Inn, 68-Clarence Inn, 69-Coach and Horses Inn, 70-Wheatsheaf, 71-White Swan Hotel, 72-Red Lion, 73-Borough Arms, 74-Angel Hotel, 75-Dog and Bull and Plume of Feathers, 76-King's Head, 77-Porter Stores, 78-Queen's Head, 79-Great George, 80-Duke of Wellington Inn, 81-Crown Inn, 82-Coach and Horses, 83-Cardiff Arms, 84-Earl Grey Inn, 85-Black Horse, 86-Boar's Head, 87-Swan Hotel, 88-Tanner's Arms, 89-Castle Stores Inn, 90-Black Horse, 91-Two Reformers Inn, 92-Unicorn Inn, 93-Bridge End Inn, 94-Abergavenny Hotel, 95-Belmont Inn, 96-Great Western Hotel, 97-Tithe Barn, 98-Gate House, 99-New Fountain Inn, 100-Nag's Head, 101-London Hotel, 102-Omar Pasha, 103-Monmouthshire House, 104-Globe, 105-County Club, 106-Victoria Inn, 107-New Market Inn, 108-Royal Oak, 109-Farmer's Arms, 110-Black Lion, 111-Greyhound Vaults, 112-Facey's Brewery, 113-Market Tavern.

Introduction

The earliest known innkeeper in Abergavenny was William Lloyd of the Golden Lion in 1591 or 1592. Innkeepers recorded in the seventeenth century include Valentine Thomas (1677), John William (1682) and James James (1688). Unfortunately, we do not know the names or whereabouts of any of their inns.

In 1686, Thomas Lewis, innholder, left all his worldly goods 'unto Jane my deere and loveing wife'. He did not actually die until June 1696 and the inventory of his possessions made then gives an excellent impression of a late seventeenth-century inn. The house was obviously large and comfortable – it contained nine bedsteads, eight feather beds with bolsters and rugs, brass and pewter valued at £2 and 'table clothes table napkins and other linnen' worth £1 15s. The inn was stocked with beer, ale and cider worth £1 10s and two fletches of bacon. The beer and ale were brewed on the premises – there were 40lbs of 'ready made malt', one 'great brueing kettle' and 'hogssheads kilderkins and other vessels' to hold the finished product. A kilderkin is an 18-gallon cask; a hogshead holds 54 gallons. Another will, dated 1799, mentions Matthew Mase, innholder, though again without naming his premises.

The 1780s saw strenuous efforts on the part of the government to clamp down on unruly public houses. In June 1787, George III issued a royal proclamation for 'the Encouragement of piety and Virtue and for preventing and punishing of Vice, profaneness and Immorality'. As a result, the Monmouthshire justices of the peace resolved that innkeepers applying for a licence should produce annual certificates 'of their Good behaviour and the Good Order of their Houses' signed by the vicar and churchwardens of their parish. Shortly afterwards, the Abergavenny Vestry Committee certified that:

> the Undermentioned Publicans ... are of good Fame, Sober life & Conversation & ... are Qualified in every respect to keep a Publick House.

There follows a list of thirty-one public houses whose licensees met with the approval of 'the Minister, Churchwardens and principal Inhabitants' who sat on the Vestry Committee!

A valuable source of trade for local publicans in the first half of the nineteenth century was the growth in popularity of friendly or benefit societies. These were formed to provide mutual insurance for their members in time of sickness or distress. The members met regularly in the public houses and paid subscriptions into a fund which could be drawn on for financial help when need arose.

The earliest men's society was established at the White Swan in 1794, followed by others at the London Apprentice in 1808 and the Unicorn in 1815. The 1820s saw the greatest growth in their popularity and men's societies were established at the Bull Inn, the Sun Inn, and the New Swan. 1841 saw the founding of the society at the Crown Inn and the last society to be set up was at the King's Arms in 1851. Women's societies were founded at the Old Duke in 1814, at the New Swan in 1829 and the London Apprentice in 1852.

It is obvious that local publicans vied with each other to secure the extra trade a friendly society could bring, and societies quite often switched their allegiance from pub to pub. The women's society established at the New Swan in 1829 moved to the Unicorn in 1832, from there to the King's Arms in 1849 and from there to the King's Head in 1852. The men's society set up at the Bull Inn in 1823 moved to the King's Head in 1837 and then to the Old Duke in 1863.

The early nineteenth century also saw another important development, with the creation of beerhouses by the Beer Act of 1830, which was aimed at reducing public drunkenness by weaning the public off gin. Under the Act, any householder who paid the Poor Rate could sell beer, ale and cider by taking out an excise licence granted by the Excise authorities on payment of two guineas. Beerhouses were licensed for six days a week (excluding Sundays) and could not sell wine or spirits. Many of the fully licensed pubs in Abergavenny began as simple beerhouses. These included the Black Lion, the Belmont Inn, the Market Tavern and the Omar Pasha. In total, around fifty-one beerhouse keepers are recorded in Abergavenny at various times in the nineteenth century.

The first half of the nineteenth century was also the golden age of the stagecoach. These lightly built vehicles were the only sure way of covering large distances in a fairly short time and Abergavenny boasted no less than three coaching inns: the Angel in Cross Street; the Greyhound in High Street and the George Inn in Frogmore Street. By 1829, the Angel was a posting inn and office for the mail coaches to London, Milford Haven, Newport, Bristol and Merthyr, and also coaches for Birmingham, Shrewsbury and Aberystwyth. In 1835, the *Fusileer* stagecoach left the George for Brecon and Bristol, the *Telegraph* for Hereford and the *Royal Mail* for Merthyr. From the Greyhound, the *Paul Pry* ran to London and Carmarthen daily, while the *Tally-Ho* made for Merthyr on Tuesdays and Saturdays. The stagecoaches were effectively killed off by the coming of the railway in the 1850s.

Prior to the nineteenth century, most pubs in Abergavenny brewed their own beer in the brewhouse on the premises but the 1820s saw the growth of local breweries, which soon saw the potential of buying up public houses to increase their sales. The first brewery in Abergavenny was the Phoenix Brewery built by William Morgan in Lion Street in 1823. He soon set about acquiring pubs. He loaned money to the landlord of the Prince Albert in Baker Street and is recorded as the owner of no less than seven pubs and beerhouses at various times: the Bull Inn, the Market House Tavern, the Lion Street Tavern, the Angler's Arms, the Blorenge Inn and two beerhouses in Lion Street.

William Morgan was soon followed by William Ellis, who started out in 1825 as the owner of the Dragon's Head. He took out the lease on Isaac Wyke's new brewery in Lion Street in February 1827 and, by 1839, was building the Royal Victoria Brewery in Baker Street. At the same time, he became the owner of the Vine Tree and he was later to buy the Britannia on the tramroad from Nantyglo to the canal wharf at Llanwenarth.

By far the largest and most successful of the local brewers was Samuel Henry Facey. He started as a wine and spirit merchant in Cross Street in 1864 and opened his own brewery in Market Street sometime between 1873 and 1875. As early as 1873, Facey had bought the Bush Inn in Tudor Street and he is listed as the owner of the Tanner's Arms in 1880. By 1950, Facey's owned no less than thirteen pubs in the district.

Another successful local brewer was Thomas Delafield. He had started out as a beer retailer in Tudor Street in 1862. By January 1864, he was the publican of the King's Arms. By 1873, he had bought the King's Arms outright and was running his own brewery at the rear of the premises. He and his family ran several other pubs and off-licences in the town, including the Sun Inn in Cross Street, No. 71 St Helen's Road and No. 55 Union Road. From 1884 until 1914, his son, Thomas Alfred Delafield, owned the Monmouthshire House in Ross Road.

A prominent out-of-town brewer was Charles Edwards of Llanfoist. Edwards' Llanfoist Brewery had been established around 1850 on the site between St Faith's church and the main road through the village. By 1873, Edwards had acquired James Jones' brewery in Nevill Street and, in 1897, he added the Bridge End Inn to his holdings. By 1914, the brewery also owned the Cantref Inn, the North Western Hotel, the Sun Inn, the Market Tavern, the Vine Tree and the Belle Vue in North Street. In 1928, the Britannia was added to the list and, by 1938, the brewery had also bought the Butcher's Arms and the Farmer's Arms. By 1945, the brewery owned around fifty houses in and around Abergavenny. In the same year, the business was bought up by Andrew Buchan's Rhymney Brewery and the Llanfoist Brewery was closed. In 1949, Buchan's started a soft-drinks factory at the site, under the name of Llanfoist Table Waters Ltd.

Keeping the pubs themselves also tended to run in families. From 1787 to 1791, Valentine Trew was at the Royal Oak in Lion Street. In the nineteenth century, William Trew is recorded as the publican of the Three Tuns (1839-42), the Bridgend Inn (1859-65) and the Clarence Inn (1859-62), and as the owner of the Hen and Chickens (1868-73). In 1851, William had married Elizabeth Herbert, the owner of the London Apprentice, and so had added that pub to his licensed empire. He was also a butcher!

Another family of publicans was the Denners. The tribal tradition started with Joseph Denner, who ran the Three Tuns (1852-53). Thomas Denner was landlord of the Cooper's Arms (1871) and the Farmer's Arms (1873-77), while John Denner was at the Forester's Arms (1868-91) and the Beaufort Arms (1895-1914). A little later, William Denner is recorded at the White Swan in 1901 and the George Hotel in Frogmore Street in 1906. These were later taken over by Mrs Rosa Denner, who ran the White Swan from 1913 until 1934 and the George between 1910 and 1920. Later still, the Sun Inn was run by Sarah Denner in 1926 and by William Denner from 1927 onwards. Coincidentally, this family was also engaged in the butchery business.

However, respectable opinion did not always approve of public houses. In February 1872, the *Abergavenny Chronicle* was much opposed to the movement to limit the working day of ordinary people to nine hours. One of the reasons for this attitude was the belief that the working class would only waste the extra free hour a day at their disposal:

> the larger portion of our artisans spend their evenings at the public house ... it is but natural to suppose that the extra hour per day will oftener be spent in the taproom over the pipe and glass than anywhere else.

In August 1897, Police Superintendent J. Davies reported that:

> The population of the town of Abergavenny, according to the last census, is 7,640, and there are 51 alehouses and beerhouses on premises, and 4 beer off premises. Thus showing that there is one licensed house to each 121 inhabitants.

By the time of the First World War, the power of breweries was growing. In May 1914, no fewer than thirty-one of the fifty-two public houses and off-licences in Abergavenny were owned by breweries. The local brewers led the way – Charles Edwards' brewery in Llanfoist headed the table with six houses, closely followed by Facey's and Delafield's with five each. The Rhymney Brewery owned the White Horse and the London Hotel, and the Brecon Brewery had the Old Duke and the Forester's Arms. Also by this time, John Owen Marsh, the proprietor of the Great Western Hotel, had added the Rothesay and the Belmont Inn to his holdings.

However, brewers from further afield had also been busily acquiring houses. They included the Hereford and Tredegar Brewery (the Great George), Arnold Perett & Co. of Hereford (the King's Head, the Albert and the Blue Bell), the Alton Court Brewery of Ross (the Cross Keys) and two Bristol firms, Garton & Co. and W.J. Rogers & Co., owned the Mount Pleasant and the Grofield respectively. By 1938, Ind Coope of Burton upon Trent had acquired the Old Herefordshire House, John Owen Marsh had sold his properties to Hancocks Ltd of Cardiff, and Hall's Brewery of Oxford had acquired the Station Hotel. The number of pubs owned by breweries had risen to thirty-seven out of forty-six licensed premises and, of these, twenty-four were in the hands of out-of-town breweries.

Mr Charles Price (a lifelong inhabitant of Nevill Street) had vivid memories of the effects of the brewers' products:

> The ale that was produced in the 1920s I'm sure was a much stronger brew than today's beer. Most weekends a fight would break out in St John's Square or Tudor Street and at holiday weekends it was a dead cert there would be more than one. It was mostly between men, but on rare occasions it was the women who were the attackers.

However, pubs had other roles to play and, as Charles Price also records in his memoirs, market days were especially busy:

> In the 1920s there were very few cars, so farmers and their wives came in by horse and trap... Many of the public houses and hotels, such as the Greyhound and the Swan accommodated the horses and the traps or carts were left in various yards or on the road outside the pubs. Cross Street particularly on the east side had many traps parked one behind the other practically the whole length of the road. All the pubs and hotels also had market rooms with an attendant to which shopkeepers could send parcels and goods bought by the farmers' wives who would collect them at the end of the day.

Acknowledgements

This book grew out of an exhibition held at Abergavenny Museum in 1990. The exhibition came about as the result of a heated discussion among the regulars of the Hen and Chickens regarding the number of pubs there had once been in Tudor Street. I hope that a copy of this book will now sit behind every bar in Abergavenny to settle such amicable disputes!

I would like to thank Rachael Rogers, the curator of Abergavenny Museum, and Barbara Bartl, her documentation assistant, for their patience and perseverance! My thanks are also due to the staff at the Gwent Record Office and the National Library of Wales for all their help and assistance. Special thanks are due to Mr Louis Bannon for permission to use the photographs on pages 19, 43, 52, 55, 57, 65, 85, 96, 101 and 125, and to Sally Davis for the maps. All other photographs are from the Abergavenny Museum collections.

I would also like to thank everyone at Tempus for all their patience and hard work and, finally, Wendy for putting up with me!

Abergavenny Pubs

BAKER STREET
Baker Street was built to connect Tudor Street with Frogmore Street in 1839.

THE GROFIELD INN, NO. 23, BAKER STREET
In the words of 'an Abergavenny Octogenarian' in 1880:

> The first houses that were built on the Grofield were the Grofield Inn and the house adjoining.

That was in 1839 and the first landlord was a Mr Prothero. The pub's rateable value at that time was £22. In March 1859, the then publican, James Webb, is recorded as having 'left the town', though the reason for his departure is not stated!

From 1860 to 1865, the publican was Joseph Brown, who had also been the landlord of the King's Arms (1849-1852) and the King's Head (1854-1859).

Samuel Peers (or Pearce), who ran the Grofield in the mid-1870s, married Eliza, the widow of John Symes of the Railway Hotel in Brecon Road (see below). He is described by one of Symes' sons, Henry, in a letter dated 22 August 1874, as 'a proper Blackard'. John Symes had left the Railway Hotel to Eliza for the period of twelve calendar months after his death; after that it was to go to his son. Interestingly, the Rate Book for 1873 (when the Railway Hotel was in Eliza's possession) names 'Samuel Pearce' as its publican and owner! He had obviously moved in with her quite soon after John Symes' death – they were certainly married by March 1874. Henry also says of his stepmother that 'she sold Everything she possible could ... she is now Married to another by the Name of Sam Peerce and they are keeping the Grofield Inn'. This may explain Henry's opinion of him!

In November 1884, Mrs Sarah Ann Howells, the landlord's wife, gave evidence against a local sheep and cattle drover charged with stealing a box of cigars worth 5s (25p) from the bar. According to the *Abergavenny Chronicle*, the man said 'he had been drinking all day and knew nothing about the cigars'. He pleaded guilty and was given a fine of £1 or fourteen days in prison.

A tavern token in the collections of the National Museum of Wales has 'Morgan' as the landlord but no other record of a landlord of this name has yet been found. By 1914, the pub had been bought by James Rogers Brewery of Bristol.

Publicans: Mr Prothero (1839), Charles Jordan (1842-1844), William Rowley (1850, had moved to the Sun Inn by 30 May), William Sayce (May 1850-1853), Robert Purslow (1858), James Webb (1859), Joseph Brown (1860-1865), Alfred Brown (1868-1871), Thomas Sleeman (1872-1873), Samuel Peers (August

1874-1877), John Howells (1884-1891), George Lucas (1895), James W. Whitney (1901), William Powell (1906-1912), William Cook (1914), William Dulson (1923-1934), Robert Thomas (1937-1939).
Owners (when known): William Jones (1839-1868), Mrs Jones (1872-1873), James Rogers & Co. Ltd (1914-1938).

THE CARPENTER'S ARMS, NO. 11, BAKER STREET
(formerly the Prince Albert, the Salutation and the Punch Bowl)

The pub, originally known as the Prince Albert, was built by Benjamin Lewis, probably sometime between 1839 and 1845. A very interesting document in the museum collections, dated to 1861, gives detailed descriptions of the site as it appeared in 1828, 1846, 1853 and 1861.

When Benjamin Lewis acquired the site in 1828, it was a courtyard surrounded by ten cottages with access through a narrow entrance from Frogmore Street. That is how it still appeared on Wood's map of 1834. By 1839, it was known as Lewis' Court and, by 1846, some of the cottages had been demolished to make way for the laying down of Baker Street. Others had been replaced with new properties that included:

> Stable and Brewhouse ... erected by Benjn Lewis on the site of two former dwelling houses then or then late in the occupation of the said Wm Taylor

Another document in the museum, dated 21 July 1845, records how 'John Taylor of the Prince Albert, in the Town of Abergavenny, Retailer of Beer' used all 'the Goods Utensils Implements and things' in the pub to secure a loan of £21 3s 6d from 'William Morgan of Abergavenny ... Brewer and Maltster' (of the Phoenix Brewery in Lion Street). In the event of his being unable to repay the money, all the goods were to be forfeit.

For a brief period, the pub seems to have been known as the Salutation. It is recorded by that name in 1853 with Jeremiah Jacobs as landlord. However, in the first document mentioned above it is described (also in 1853) as the Prince Albert. The pub was still called the Prince Albert in 1861 when the premises were bought by the Misses Trotter who owned the nearby Royal Victoria Brewery (see below). Susan Trotter married John Broadley of Bath in 1867 and a document drawn up before their wedding refers to the pub as the Punch Bowl 'now in the occupation of Thomas Parry and George Window'. There seems to have been some confusion regarding the publican's name as the name William Parry had been crossed out and replaced by Thomas. It seems probable that both names were mistakes for the John Parry recorded in the trade directories and Rate Books. By 1869, it was known as the Carpenter's Arms. In that year, John Broadley sold the pub and the four adjoining cottages for £700 to Richard Price, grocer. At that time, the tenant was John Parry.

In July 1872, the landlord, William Fynn, was charged with permitting drunkenness on his premises. His lawyer stated that:

> [the] defendant had not kept the house long and that it was kept very orderly. – The Bench said they were pleased to hear that defendant kept the house so orderly. – Fined 20s and costs.

The pub is last listed in 1912.

Publicans: John Taylor (1845), James Watkins (1851), Martha Lewis (1852), Jeremiah Jacobs (1853), Isaac Thomas (1860), Hannah Havard (1862), John Parry (1865-1871), William Fynn (1872), Henry J. Watkins (1873-1906), Richard Richards (1910), listed 1912.

Owners (when known): Benjamin Lewis (1828-1860), Emma and Susan Trotter (1861-1868), John Broadley (1869), Richard Price (1869-1872).

THE ROYAL VICTORIA BREWERY, NO. 13, BAKER STREET
(*see* Lion Street)

Before acquiring the Dragon's Head in Nevill Street from his future father-in-law in 1825, William Ellis was a simple yeoman (*see* Nevill Street). He began his career as a brewer by leasing Isaac Wyke's new brewery in Lion Street in February 1827. By 1839, he was building on a plot of land near the Grofield Inn in Baker Street and, shortly after, opened a new brewery there known as the Royal Victoria Brewery. In February 1841, he and Nicholas Price, 'brewer, of Abergavenny', bought the Britannia 'adjoining the Tram Road or Railway of Messrs Bailey leading from Nant y Glo to the Wharf near the Canal at Llanwenarth' from Roger Phillip of Gelli Felen, 'Innholder', for five shillings. In 1880, 'an Abergavenny Octogenarian' recalled that:

This Mr Ellis lived at the Lower Pentre, and one night, on his way home, he fell off his horse, and dislocated his neck, and was killed.

The old Royal Victoria Brewery in Baker Street.

A Royal Victoria Brewery billhead from 1852 – 'To Her Majesty by Appointment'!

In fact, William Ellis' horse had taken fright and bolted as the *Paul Pry* stagecoach hurtled along the Brecon Road on its way to Carmarthen from the Greyhound.

William Ellis was still at the brewery in April 1852. He is described in a receipt of that date as 'Ale and Porter Brewer to Her Majesty by Appointment'. By July 1853, the brewery was in the hands of Francis Turfrey and Co. It seems likely therefore that William Ellis fell off his horse sometime between April 1852 and July 1853. Francis Turfrey also lived at the Lower Pentre (now known as Pentre Court) and is recorded as bankrupt in 1855.

In September 1854, Mary Ellis, William's widow, assigned the brewery to Samuel Trotter. Trotter had begun brewing in Monk Street by 1842 and seems to have retained his interest in the business there for some time, certainly until 1862. By then, he had retired and the business had passed to his daughters, Susan and Emma, who employed a manager at the Royal Victoria by the name of Henry John Higginson. By 1865, Higginson had been replaced by John Dawes and the brewery was known as the Abergavenny Brewery.

In January 1867, the brewery passed to Nathaniel Cook and reverted to its original name. Nathaniel seems to have fallen into financial difficulties, as his water was cut off the following year. In 1871, the owner was Joseph Cooke.

From July 1872, the owner is recorded as Edward Phillips, though by 1880 he had moved on to the Tyne Brewery in Newcastle-upon-Tyne. The owner in 1884 was James Gough and the business was once again known as the Royal Victoria. Gough also owned the freehold on the Old Fountain Inn in Frogmore Street. He put the brewery on the market in 1888 and the sale particulars give a very detailed description of the premises:

> spacious covered yard, capable of stowing 500 empty barrels with ample room for drays and other purposes, Malt House with cistern capable of wetting 15 quarters; Store Rooms with malt bins capable of holding 600 sacks of malt. The Brewery comprises: Tun Rooms, Water Tank, Stores, extraordinarily large and compact Cellars, Hop-rooms, and every other requisite building for carrying on an extensive Malting and Brewing business; also a well with a never failing supply of water, worked by a steam pump

There was also the manager's house, another house 'suitable for a foreman', two dray houses, stabling for twelve horses, a coachhouse and two harness rooms.

In November 1896, Edwin Morse, the then owner, leased part of the premises out to the Conservative Club. Another brewer, Charles James Powell, is listed under 'Grofield' in 1852 but the location of his business is not known.

BRECON ROAD
In the 1830s and 1840s, the stretch of the Brecon Road between the junctions with St Michael's Road and Chapel Road was known as New Road. However, as several other 'new' roads are referred to, it is sometimes difficult to decide which one is meant (see New Road). It is first called Brecon Road in 1852.

THE NORTH WESTERN TEMPERANCE HOTEL, NO. 1, BRECON ROAD
(*see* Brecon Road Brewery)

THE STATION HOTEL, NO. 37, BRECON ROAD

In 1859 and 1860, this site was occupied by a house and garden in the tenancy of James Powell. The earliest record of the Station Hotel dates back to 1865, when a Mr Frederick Phillips was the publican.

In January 1901, Mary Hannah Clarke left the pub to Robert Newton in trust for her daughter, Hilda Mary. In 1912, Hilda turned twenty-one and so became the proud owner of the Station Hotel. The *Cardiff, Newport and District Trade Directory* for 1912 advertises the pub as 'the noted house in the district for Oxford Beer and Stout; cigars of the best quality; accommodation for cyclists'.

By September 1938, the pub had been bought up by Hall's Brewery of Oxford.

Publicans: Frederick Phillips (1865), Miss Alden (1868), William Boycott (1871), William Bettridge (1872-1877), John Joseph Clarke (1884-1895), Mrs Mary Hannah Clarke (1901), Mr Woodward (1905), Joseph Wordsworth (1906-1926), Mrs Isabel Wordsworth (1934), Samuel Edwards (1937-1939).
Owners (when known): Francis Evans (1868-1873), Mary Hannah Clarke (1901, died 27 January 1901), Robert Newton (January 1901-June 1912), Hilda Mary Clarke (1912), Henry Thomas (1914), Hall's Brewery Ltd (1938).

THE RAILWAY HOTEL, NO. 32, BRECON ROAD

(formerly the White Hart and the London and North Western Railway Hotel)
The earliest record of a pub by the name of the White Hart in Abergavenny dates to 1834 when the 'White Hart public house in Tudor Street' is listed in the will of Revd Richard William Payne Davies of Cwrt y Gollen. Whether this is the same house as the White Hart in what is now called the Brecon Road is uncertain.

In October 1840, John Symes, wheelwright, took out a 99-year lease on a plot of land called 'Lower Groffield' from Baker Gabb at £14 per annum. By July 1842, he had built a wheelwright's shop, a carpenter's shop and six houses known as Symes' Row (now Nos 24-32a Commercial Street).

Despite the fact that the pub stood at the end of Symes' Row, John Symes is not actually recorded as the publican of the White Hart until 1850. In 1853, the pub's rateable value stood at £8.

The pub is first referred to as the Railway Hotel in May 1865. To finance all this building work, John Symes had borrowed heavily and, by 1865, the pub was mortgaged to Isaac Isaacs, a pawnbroker in Frogmore Street, to the tune of £800. This is probably why the 1868 Rate Book lists Isaac Isaacs as the owner! Towards the end of his life, John Symes was involved in a five-year lawsuit in Chancery with George Hughes of Penpergwm over the estate of a Mrs Maddox, which cost him £200 and which his son blamed for shortening his life.

It is obvious from the family papers in the museum that there was a great deal of tension between John Symes' wife, Eliza, and his children by a previous marriage, Henry, Charles and Sarah. John died on 28 January 1872 and left the pub to his wife for a year. Thereafter it was to go to his Henry, on condition that he pay £140 to his younger brother, Charles, who had emigrated to Australia.

Interestingly, the Rate Book for 1873 names Samuel Pearce as both publican and owner of the Railway Hotel. He obviously moved in with Eliza quite soon after John Symes' death. When Henry sold the pub to Thomas Griffiths, a Tredegar innkeeper, in 1877, the new owner had to pay Charles his £140 plus £24 15s 2d interest.

Between around 1884 and 1910, the pub was called the London and North Western Railway Hotel but by 1914 it was once again known as the Railway Hotel.

For many years, the Railway held a special licence to allow railway employees coming off the night shift at 6 a.m. to enjoy a tot of whisky on their way home from work! The Abergavenny Borough Band practised here for many years, usually in the cellar. Later, the pub was taken over by Facey's Brewery (*see* Market Street).

Publicans: John Symes (1850-28 January 1872, though James Brice appears as publican in the trade directory for 1865), Samuel Pearce (1873), Benjamin Twigger (1875), John Morgan (1877), William Saunders (1880), John Evans (1884-1895), David Wynne Morgan (1901), Daniel Davies (1906), Frederick Auty (1910), Levi Rogers (1914-1923), Ben Evans (1926), Edward Ashcroft (1934), John Richard Jones (1937), W. Jones (1938-1939).
Owners (when known): John Symes (May 1850-28 January 1872, though Isaac Isaacs is listed as the owner once in 1868), Eliza Symes (28 January 1872-28 January 1873; Samuel Pearce is listed as owner in the 1873 Rate Book), Henry Albert Symes (28 January 1873-9 March 1877), Thomas Griffiths (9 March 1877), S.H. Facey Ltd (1914-1939).

THE CANTREF INN, NO. 61, BRECON ROAD

In 1843, the plot of land on which the Cantref Inn now stands was a grassy meadow of 1 acre and 2 perches, owned by the Duke of Beaufort and rented by William Rowley. He later entered into a very varied career as an innkeeper and is recorded at the Grofield Inn (1850), the Sun Inn (1850-1858), the Market Tavern (1859) and the Cow Inn (1860-1865).

A Cantreff Arms is recorded at the Monmouth Road end of Mill Street in 1859 but by 1860 it had changed its name to the Angler's Arms. The earliest record of the Brecon Road Cantref Inn dates to 1868, with Samuel Munn Jones as the first known publican.

By the time of the First World War, the pub was owned by Charles Edwards' brewery of Llanfoist.

The Cantref Inn, pictured in the Burrow's Guide of 1903.

Publicans: Samuel Munn Jones (1868-1875), A.T.E. Davies (1876), Charles Pritchard (1877), Richard Briscoe (1884), Philip Henry Price (1891-1901), Frederick T. Tipton (1906-1914), Joseph Baron (1923-1926), Harold John Jones (1934-1939).
Owners (when known): Walter Morgan (1868-1880), Charles Edwards Ltd (1914-1938).

THE NORTH WESTERN HOTEL, NO. 26, BRECON ROAD
(formerly the Collier's Arms)
The pub is first recorded in 1871 as a beerhouse run by George Pritchard, 'beer retailer and coal merchant'. By 1876 it was known, appropriately enough, as the Collier's Arms. It is first referred to as the North Western in 1884.

A local resident recalls that during the First World War, the landlord was Captain Harry Powell of the Abergavenny fire brigade: 'If there was a fire on, he would turn the engine round if he didn't have his medals on'. The last known landlord was a Mr North. The pub partially burnt down in 1968 and became a private residence.

Publicans: George Pritchard (1871-1895), Alfred Parry (1901), John Dusting (1906), John Watson Barnfield (1910-1912), George B. Hambling (1914), Henry C. Powell (1923), Evan Evans (1934), William J. Hancock (1937-1938), William Eccles (1939).
Owners: Charles Edwards Ltd (1914-1939).

THE BRECON ROAD BREWERY, NO. 1, BRECON ROAD
The Brecon Road Brewery started life as the carrier's office of Thomas Haines and Co. (1842-1850). The brewery was certainly in business by 1871, when the owner, Frank Morgan, entered into a brief partnership with Samuel Henry Facey (*see* Cross Street, Market Street) which was still going in July 1872.

The North Western Hotel (marked with a cross) and, opposite, the Station Hotel in 1912.

The former Brecon Road Brewery, c. 1925.

One of his bills in the museum collections describes Frank Morgan as 'Maltster and Brewer, Agent for Dublin Stout and Ind Coope and Co.'s Burton Ales'. It also makes clear that the brewery was in business between July 1880 and February 1881. In those days, a firkin of XX cost 9s. Frank Morgan is last listed there in 1884. By 1891, the brewery was being managed by William Morris Jenkins.

Between 1891 and 1901, the building is listed as the North Western Temperance Hotel run by Joseph Edwards (1891) and George Hand (1895-1901).

REYNOLDS AND WASE'S BREWERY, NOS 33-35, BRECON ROAD
Reynolds and Wase, brewers, are listed in the trade directories in 'New Road' between 1842 and 1844. They are also recorded in the 1843 tithe schedule as a tenant of Baker Gabb. The Abergavenny Tithe Map shows the site quite clearly (plot 429) on the site now occupied by Heronhurst, next door to the Station Hotel.

By 1850, the premises had been taken over by William Newman (listed as Thomas Newman in 1850 and 1858), hop and cider merchant, who is recorded there until 1873. Henry Symes' letter to his brother in Australia, dated 22 August 1874, mentions the fact that 'old Newman is dead'.

BEERHOUSES (LOCATIONS UNKNOWN)
John Morgan (1862 and 1877). There is a John Morgan recorded as living in the property next door to William Newman's cider merchant's in 1873. This would now be No. 31, Brecon Road.

John Phillips, beer retailer and trainer (1865).

CASTLE STREET

THE ANGEL HOTEL TAP, LOWER CASTLE STREET
This pub is recorded only once, in 1862.

Publicans: Joseph Saunders (1862).

THE COACH AND HORSES INN, NO.11, CASTLE STREET

The Coach and Horses is first listed as a simple beerhouse in 1835, with Joseph Cole as publican. At that time, the address is given as Angel Lane. The pub is first referred to by name in 1839. On census night, 8 June 1841, it was occupied by Joseph (35), his wife Elizabeth (29) and their children Thomas (12), Amelia (5), Henry (1) and Emma (1).

On 14 November 1888, Evan Jones of Maerdy Park, 'Gentleman', leased the pub to Robert William Miller, a brewer from Hereford, for an annual rent of £45. The Mrs Williams mentioned in the lease as the sitting tenant is probably the Ann Williams listed as publican in 1884.

On 4 May 1894, a detailed inventory was drawn up of all the furniture, fittings and stock being sold to Mr Henry Nicholas ('the ingoing tenant') by Mr Benjamin Tomkins ('the outgoing tenant'); they were valued at £120 2s. The list gives us a detailed picture of a late Victorian public house. The premises had a smoking room and a bar. The smoking room fittings included a piano, two portraits and ten cast-iron spitoons! The bar had only five spitoons ('one broken') but also boasted an aquarium, a glass-backed dresser, a stuffed owl, a 'pictorial view of the world' and a 'breeding cage and two birds'. Among the pastimes catered for were draughts, cribbage, dominos and a 'ring board and rings' for bar quoits. There were also six bedrooms, a parlour, kitchen, pantry, stable and backyard, passage and stairs. For a period during 1903, Thomas Meredith was the publican on a temporary licence.

Publicans: Joseph Cole (1835-1841), George Leach (1842-1844), Charles Powles (1850), Charles Palmer (1852-1853), Thomas Morgan (1858-1860), William Williams (1862), James Williams (1864-1877), Mrs Ann Williams (1884-1888), Charles Jenkins (1891), Benjamin Tomkins (1894), Henry Nicholas (1894-1895), Ambrose Powell (1901), Thomas Meredith (1903), Thomas Pollard (1906), William Jones (1910-1914), Thomas Doman (May 1914), Francis Thomas (1923-1934), William Davies (1937), ? Grant (1938), M. Powell (1939).

Owners (when known): William James (1839-1860), J.T. Hands (1864), Evan Jones (1868-1888), Robert William Miller (1888, leaseholder), William Jones (1914), Arnold Perret & Co. Brewers (1938).

THE CLARENCE INN, NO. 23, CASTLE STREET

The earliest record of the Clarence Inn is found in an inventory 'of Fixtures and Goods taken by Mr Joseph Morgan from Mr Wm Prosser at the Clarence Inn in Castle Street in Abergavenny, the 27th day of March 1856', which records that the pub's bar contained '5 Hull Engines and Pipes' worth £23. Beer was obviously being pulled from pumps at the bar, rather than brought from the cask in jugs.

In March 1858, William Prosser, mason, leased the pub to James Taylor for £19 19s 0d annually. He agreed to keep it 'as an Inn or Public House and will keep and conduct the same in a proper and orderly manner'. At that time, the bar contained 'Two benches, One Short Settle, Nest of Shelves, Counter with Marble Slab, Three Beer Engines, Bell pull'. Between 1858 and 1859, it seems to have passed from Ann Chapman (listed in *Slater's Trade Directory*) to William Trew (recorded in the Poor Rate Book).

In May 1872, the landlady, Mrs Alicia Abraham, was charged with 'allowing drunkenness' on her premises. Two tailors, George McCarthy (who lodged at the pub) and a Mr Holland, acted as witnesses on Mrs Abraham's behalf and eventually the charges were dismissed.

The pub stopped trading sometime between 1877 and 1880. It is described merely as Clarence House in the 1880 electoral register (the occupier then was a John Lewis) and is listed in the 1884 *Kelly's Directory* as a lodging house run by Mrs Ellen Lewis.

The former Clarence Inn, which had fallen on hard times in the 1970s!

Publicans: Joseph Morgan (1856), James Taylor (March 1858), Ann Chapman (1858), William Trew (1859-1864), John Vaughan (1865), W. Abraham (1868), Mrs Alicia Abraham (1871-July 1872), Miss Lewis (1873), Mrs Mary Lewis (1875-1877).
Owners (when known): William Prosser (1856-1860), William Richards (1864-July 1872), the Earl of Abergavenny (1873).

THE BEEHIVE INN, NO. 50, CASTLE STREET

The pub is first recorded in 1839, with Richard Headford as publican. At that time, it stood next to the Independent minister's manse, on the site now occupied by the chapel schoolroom and the Castle Court funeral home. By 1852, the name had passed to John Smith's beerhouse at No. 50, Castle Street, which had been in business since at least 1850. It is last recorded in January 1864.

From 1852 onwards, John Smith also ran a malthouse next door to the pub and, from 1856 on, had another one at No. 65, Castle Street. Even though the Beehive seems to have closed sometime in 1864 or 1865, John Smith is still recorded as a maltster in Castle Street until 1873. Smith owned all of what was later to be known as Castle Terrace (Nos 40-50 Castle Street). The whole block was mortgaged to John Astbury in October 1866 and, although John Smith died in December 1873, his widow, Mary Ann Smith, was still living in No. 50 in February 1876. In 1880, 'an Abergavenny Octogenarian' recorded his memories of the place:

> At one time Tudor-street was one of the principal streets in the town. All the butchers' shops, with one exception, that of George Leonard's, which was at the Beehive public house, in Castle-street, were in that street. The Beehive has been discontinued as an alehouse within recent years; but at one time – when the sheep market was where the Girls' and Infants' National Schools are – the house did a capital business.

Publicans: Richard Headford (1839-1840), John Smith (1850-1864).
Owners (when known): John Powell (1839-1840), 'late T.A. Gabb' (1850), 'late J. Gabb' (1853), J.A. Gabb (1856), J.T. Gabb (1859), J.T.G. Gabb (1860), Revd J.T. Gabb (1864).

Castle Street in the 1950s. The former Beehive Inn is the large building on the extreme right.

THE NEW DUKE INN, NO. 56, CASTLE STREET
(formerly the Castle Inn, the Globe and the Duke of York Inn)

The Duke of York is first recorded in 1822, with John Leng as publican. The pub is first called the New Duke Inn in May 1850, with Thomas Symonds as publican. He changed the name to the Globe and the next landlord, John Morgan Edmunds, stuck with it. Another pub of the same name is recorded in Monk Street in 1852, being run by a John Lloyd.

On 2 June 1852, a housewarming supper and ball ('tickets eighteen pence each, supper on the table at nine o'clock') were held to celebrate the arrival of the new landlord, Enoch Lloyd Cooper. He changed the name to the Castle Inn.

By 1853, it was once again known as the Duke of York Inn. By 1865, it is listed once again as the New Duke. Though the pub had closed by 1871, another Globe is listed in Castle Street in 1906 and 1910.

In November 1890, the building opened as the town's first cottage hospital and it fulfilled that role until the new Victoria Cottage Hospital was opened in Hereford Road in 1902.

In June 1892, the building 'formerly known as the Duke of York Inn, but now known as the Cottage Hospital' was put up for sale at the Greyhound Hotel by Messrs Straker and Son. At that time, the rent for 'the Cottage Hospital, with the Garden and Summer House' was £28 per annum.

Publicans: John Leng (1822–died 1841), John Pye (1842-1844), Thomas Symonds (May 1850), John Morgan Edmunds (May 1851-1852), Enoch Lloyd Cooper (1852), Henry C. Williams (1853), William Roberts (1859-1860), Mrs Ann Edwards (1862-1864), Henry Morgan (1865-1868), Thomas Pollard (1906), W. Jones (1910).

Owners (when known): 'late William Williams' (1839), Mary Williams (1840), 'late Williams' (1850-1851), Elizabeth Lewis (1853-1856), E.G. Lewis (1859-1868), Miss Lewis (1872).

THE OLD DUKE INN, NO. 57, CASTLE STREET
(also known as The Duke of Cumberland Inn)

Prior to its demolition in 1962, the Old Duke stood on the site opposite the service entrance to the

The New Duke (left) and the Old Duke (centre), 1957.

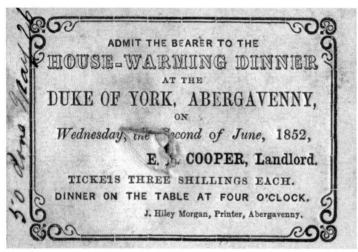

ADMIT THE BEARER TO THE

HOUSE-WARMING DINNER

AT THE

DUKE OF YORK, ABERGAVENNY,

ON

Wednesday, the second of June, 1852,

E. L. COOPER, Landlord.

TICKETS THREE SHILLINGS EACH.

DINNER ON THE TABLE AT FOUR O'CLOCK.

J. Hiley Morgan, Printer, Abergavenny.

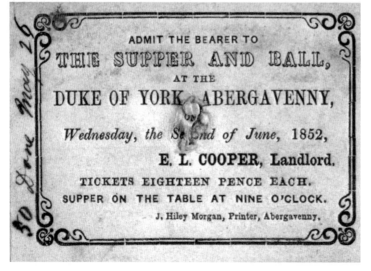

ADMIT THE BEARER TO

THE SUPPER AND BALL,

AT THE

DUKE OF YORK, ABERGAVENNY,

ON

Wednesday, the Second of June, 1852,

E. L. COOPER, Landlord.

TICKETS EIGHTEEN PENCE EACH.

SUPPER ON THE TABLE AT NINE O'CLOCK.

J. Hiley Morgan, Printer, Abergavenny.

Above and left: *Tickets to a housewarming dinner, supper and ball at the Duke of York in 1852.*

present post office. The Duke was a solid stone-built building dating from the period 1550-1600. The stone-flagged lounge was of exceptional interest, with a massive stone fireplace, oak stud and panel partition and a late Tudor doorframe. The upper floor was approached by winding stone steps.

The earliest record of the building's use as a 'tavern and public house' dates back to 1787, when a Mr Price was listed as the publican.

In 1814, a Society of Women was formed at 'the dwelling house of Alice Prosser known by the sign of the Old Duke'. The members were to meet once a month between seven and nine in the evening and to contribute at each meeting 'ten pence towards raising a fund for the good of the society and two pence to be spent'. This fund was to benefit 'the sick and helpless only', with an express rule that no 'interesting event' was to be considered as coming under that head. There were severe penalties for 'giving a sister member the lie', for using bad language, for introducing a male (husband or otherwise!) into the clubroom and for not being 'peaceable and silent at the request of the clerk or either of the stewards'.

The regulars in the bar of the Old Duke shortly before its demolition. The man in the flat cap on the right is Duggan Thacker, the first curator of the Abergavenny Museum.

The saloon bar of the Old Duke, showing the Elizabethan fireplace and oak partition wall.

The society was still going strong in 1826, when they appointed James Jones, maltster (recorded in Nevill Street between 1822 and 1852), as their trustee. By that time, the pub was occupied by David Prosser, mason, and his wife, Elizabeth. They seem to have been there since August 1820, even though Alice Prosser is still listed as the publican in 1822. In 1828, David Prosser mortgaged the pub to the same James Jones for the sum of £400 and duly surrendered the deeds to him. Among them was a copy of the will of John Watkins 'of Abergavenny, Innholder', dated 18 May 1790; it seems likely that he was one of the past landlords of the Old Duke. If so, he was succeeded by Thomas Price, who is recorded as publican and freeholder in 1791. In 1822 and again in 1840, the pub is referred to as the Duke of Cumberland.

By 1835, the publican was Ann Barton. She died in 1839 and between 1842 and 1852 the proprietor is named as Mary Barton, possibly Ann's daughter. In the 1847 Poll Book of persons entitled to vote in a general election, George Barton is listed as residing in the 'Old Duke, Abergavenny'. He was still alive in 1860, though by then he was living in Flannel Street.

In December 1863, a benefit society that had originally been established at the King's Head moved to the Old Duke, whose landlord, James Daniels, became their new treasurer.

On 5 January 1883, the then publican, William Powell, received a rather irate letter from the Talbot & Co. Mineral Water Works of Gloucester and Monmouth stating that 'According to our Books, the Bottles and Cases, as shown below, are not yet returned... Please return them as early as possible'. The letter is preserved for posterity in the museum collections.

For thirty-nine years, from 1914 to 1953, the pub was run by the Davis family, first by Albin Davis and later by his wife, Lilian. Mr Davis' brother, Archibald, ran the Forester's Arms in Tudor Street.

Many local residents have vivid memories of the Duke. As Charles Price recalls in his memoirs of old Abergavenny, 'It was a great pity to see this rather interesting old pub go. It was a great rendezvous for men every Saturday at 12 noon'.

Left: *The Old Duke and the King's Arms (furthest away) in 1962.*

Opposite: *No. 65, Castle Street, 1957. In the eighteenth century, it was the White Swan.*

Publicans: Mr Price (1787), John Watkins (1790), Thomas Price (1791), Alice Prosser (1814-1822), David and Elizabeth Prosser (1820-1826), Thomas Barton (1830-died 1832), Ann Barton (1835-died 1839), Mary Barton (1840-1853), Evan Jones (1856), James Daniel (1858-1864), Mrs Caroline Daniel (1865-1877), William John Powell (1883-1901), John Davies (1901-1906), William Stephen Davies (1910), Daniel Harris (1914), Albert Price (1914), Albin Strugnell Davis (1914-1944), Lilian Mary Davis (1944-1953).

Owners (when known): Thomas Price (1791), Ann Barton (1839), Mary Barton (1840-1853), Evan Jones (1856-1873), Brecon Brewery Co. (1914), Hereford and Tredegar Brewery Ltd (1938).

THE WHITE SWAN, NO. 65, CASTLE STREET

Among the Baker Gabb collection of documents in the National Library of Wales, a number of documents record the existence between 1769 and 1793 of 'a messuage with a brewhouse called the White Swan' which stood in Castle Street, next to the 'gatehouse called Tudor Street Gate' and which formed a block with Bailey Baker (now Old Court). By comparing these references with the later Rate Books, it is obvious that the building referred to is No. 65, Castle Street.

The pub is not listed in the 1787 Vestry list and is described in 1794 as 'a dwelling house with brewhouse'. Between 1839 and 1853, the premises were run as a malthouse by James Jones. By 1868, the property had been bought by the Batt family, who also owned and lived in Old Court. John Smith is listed as a maltster in the house between 1856 and 1873. The 1881 census lists the building as uninhabited.

Publicans: Blanch Floyer (1778).

BEERHOUSES

John Powell's beerhouse (1839-1860) stood next door to the Independent chapel's manse, on the site now covered by the chapel schoolroom and Castle Court funeral home. Only once, in 1839, it is referred to as the Beehive.

Publicans: Richard Headford (1839), Richard Williams (1850-1851), William Price (1856).
Owners: John Powell (1839-1860).

PORTER DEALER, NO. 52, CASTLE STREET

Thomas Richards is listed as a porter dealer from the Tithe Barn in Monk Street from 1835 to 1844. By 1850, the business had moved to No. 52, Castle Street, where he is recorded until 1858.

BEERHOUSES

Other beerhouse keepers, the location of whose houses is not known, include Elizabeth Price (1842-1844).

CHAPEL ROAD

THE CIDER HOUSE, CHAPEL ROAD

This house is first recorded in 1850 as a beerhouse. The Abergavenny Tithe Map of 1843 shows the building standing in what is now Chapel Road, on the edge of the old Llanfihangel tramroad in a field owned by Mary Lewis. At various times, it was listed under 'New Road'(1850), 'Chapel Lane'(1852) and 'Suburbs'(1853). By June 1851, it had become a pub called the Cider House. It is described as a 'House, Garden & Stables' owned by Mary Lewis but with William Symmonds as publican.

A few years later, it must have been demolished to build the northern side of the Brecon Road railway station.

Publicans: William Symmonds or Symons (1850-1853).
Owners: Mary Lewis (1843-1853).

BEERHOUSES (LOCATIONS UNKNOWN)

Stephen Roberts, Chapel Mill (1871).

CHICKEN STREET

THE HORSE AND GROOM

This pub is only recorded once, in 1852. The publican was Thomas Harry but the exact whereabouts of the house are not known.

Publicans: Thomas Harry (1852).

BEER RETAILERS

Other beer retailers recorded in Chicken Street but whose exact whereabouts are unknown include Catherine Probert (1835-1844).

CROSS STREET

THE WHEATSHEAF, NO. 3, CROSS STREET

The earliest reference to the Wheatsheaf is dated 1787, when Morgan Morgans was the publican. In 1791, he is listed as Morgan Morgan. David Lewis is listed as the publican from 1822 until his death in 1855.

Although he is only listed at the Wheatsheaf in 1858, John Grout is referred to in a document dated September 1856 as being 'of Abergavenny, victualler' and it is possible that he was running the pub as early as this.

Though the house was still referred to as the Wheatsheaf Inn in 1873, by 1875 the proprietor, Mrs Charlotte Shore, is simply listed as a 'wine, spirit, ale and porter merchant'. A billhead of 1876, in which the place is referred to as the Wine and Spirit Vaults, describes her as a 'Wholesale Wine and Spirit Merchant, Maltster and Hop Factor'. Mrs Shore had taken over the business from James Shore, who seems to have died sometime between 1871 and 1873. He had run the business since at least 1862. By 1884, the pub was once again known as the Wheatsheaf.

Throughout the nineteenth century, the pub was owned by the Fludyers, a local landowning family who, from 1770 onwards, were the lords of the manor of Llanfihangel nigh Usk. In 1920, Sir Arthur Fludyer sold the property to the then publican, Samuel Price. In 1923, the pub was sold again, this time to David Edward Thomas, plumber and gas fitter. By 1933, Mr Thomas had moved on to the Cross Keys Inn in Tudor Street and he sold the Wheatsheaf to the Alton Court Brewery Co. Ltd of Ross-on-Wye for £1,600.

The Wheatsheaf Inn during alterations in 1962.

The Wheatsheaf continued trading until 1961. At that time, the Alton Court Brewery had gone into liquidation and the pub was sold for £2,625, providing no trade in beers, wines or spirits took place, for the 'benefit and protection of the neighbouring property of West Country Breweries Ltd known as the Kings Head Inn'.

Publicans: Morgan Morgans (or Morgan) (1787-1791), David Lewis (1822-died 1855 3), John Grout (September 1856?-1858), James Shore (1862-1871), Mrs Charlotte Shore (July 1872-1895), Samuel Price (1895-1923), David Edward Thomas (1923-1933), William George Moore (1934-1937), H.L. Lewis (1938-1939).
Owners (when known): Sir Samuel Fludyer (1839-1873), Sir Arthur Fludyer (1914-1920), Alton Court Brewery Ltd (1933-1961).

THE WHITE SWAN HOTEL, NO. 4, CROSS STREET
(also known as the Old Swan and the Eureka Hotel)
A deed of settlement in the County Record Office dated 18 June 1766 records 'John Jones of the White Swan in the town of Abergavenny, victualler'. Another CRO document of 20 April 1779 names 'John Jones of the town of Abergavenny, corvicer' as the eldest son and heir of 'John Jones late of the Whiteswan in Abergavenny, dec'd'. In 1787, the licensee is named as Mrs Jones. On 8 September 1794, a Society of Tradesmen and Gentlemen Farmers was formed here.

In September 1832, a second Society of Tradesmen and Gentlemen Farmers was founded at the Old Swan, with the publican, John Lewis, as treasurer. The gutter heads of the current building bear the date 1835. In that year, the pub is again referred to as the Old Swan to differentiate between it and the New Swan in Mill Street (as the bottom part of Cross Street was then known).

The White Swan in 1881, from a Facey's billhead.

From 1842 until his death in 1854, the place was run as a wine merchant's shop by John Powell Williams. He was followed by Anne Sybil Williams, 'Agent for Irish Porter and Dealer in Hops'. She was probably John Williams' widow and ran the business from 1858 to 1860.

Between 1864 and 1891, the house was owned by Samuel Henry Facey and Co. Ltd, first as a retail outlet for his wine and spirit importing business and later for his brewery in Market Street. A receipt from around 1878 describes Mr Facey as an 'Importer of Foreign Wines and Spirits, Brewer and Maltster, Agent for Burton Ales and Dublin Stout'.

They also used the cellars under the Town Hall as a bonded store from around 1873 onwards. Mr Facey is recorded as living on the premises until 1880, when he built The Elms in Belmont Road as the family home.

In 1901, the place is again referred to as the White Swan. Sometime between 1906 and 1910, the pub became known as the Eureka Hotel. When Mrs Rosa Denner took over as publican from Eustace Baker in February 1913, the house reverted to its traditional name.

In more recent times, the pub was often referred to as the Dirty Duck. It finally closed in 1972.

Publicans: John Jones (1766-1779), Mrs Jones (1787), Margaret Jones (1791), R. Fox (1822-1823), George Carver (1830), John Lewis (1832), James Chamberlain (1835), John Goodwyn (1839-1840), John Powell Williams (1842-died 1854), Anne Sybil Williams (1858-1860), Samuel Henry Facey & Co. Ltd (1864-1891), William Denner (1901), Thomas George Alden (1905-1906), Daniel Holding (1910), Eustace Baker (February 1912-January 1913), Mrs Rosa Denner (February 1913-1934), L.E. Goatman (November 1934-January 1935), Horace Jones (1937-1939).
Owners (when known): John Goodwyn (1839-1840), Edward Lewis (1850-1860), Samuel Henry Facey (1864-1891), Frank H. Facey (1914), Facey & Son Ltd (1938).

The White Swan in 1967. The pub's local nickname was the Dirty Duck.

THE RED LION, NO. 5, CROSS STREET

The pub is first recorded in 1787, with a Mr Davies as licensee. In 1836, it is referred to as 'formerly called the Red Lion'. Plans drawn at the time show the brewhouse as being next door to the privy! The pub was divided into three separate premises and became the shop of Joseph Meredith, tea dealer, grocer and chandler.

Publicans: Mr Davies (1787), Thomas Roberts (1791).
Owners (when known): Rachel Herbert (1836).

THE BOROUGH ARMS, NO. 10, CROSS STREET

(formerly the Red Lion)

For most of its history, the pub was run as a wine merchant's premises by the Gunter family. James Gunter, who started the business, was already living in the house when he bought it from James Morgan of Llanelly in 1762. By 1822, it was in the hands of William Gunter Lewis. One of his advertisements survives in the museum collections:

Cross Street, Abergavenny, W.G. Lewis having commenced business in the Wholesale Foreign and British Spirit Trade begs to solicit the favours of his Friends and the Public.

William died in 1834 and from 1835 on, the premises were owned by his widow, Elizabeth, and she ran the business herself until 1862. In 1868, she died and the business was taken over by Charles Tucker (Charles Tucker and Son after 1889), who also owned No. 21 Monk Street (the Nag's Head) and the Great George. They ran the wine merchant's until 1891.

By 1895, the shop had become the Red Lion. However, from 1899 until it closed in 1907, the pub was known as the Borough Arms to commemorate the restoration of the Borough Charter. The

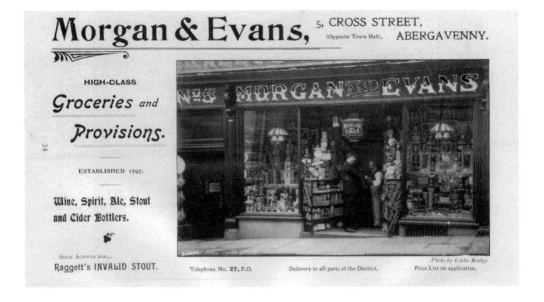

The former Red Lion in 1903.

Looking down Cross Street, c. 1905. The Borough Arms is on the right by the gas lamp.

place was put up for sale in 1905 but the solicitors, Gabb & Stafford, seem to have experienced some difficulties. In a letter dated 27 July 1905, they wrote:

> While I should be glad to oblige you in any matter as far as possible I cannot be running about for the purchaser of the 'Boro' Arms.

Wine Merchants: James Gunter (*c.*1730-1750), William Gunter Lewis (1822-died 1834), Elizabeth Gunter Lewis (1835-1853), William Saunders (1860), Charles Tucker (1868-1889), Charles Tucker and Son (1889-1891).
Publicans: Joseph Chivers (1895), Timothy Green-Jones (1901), David E. Humphries (1906).
Owners (when known): James Gunter (1762), Elizabeth Gunter (1773), William Gunter (1780), James Gabriel (1780-1787), Ann Negri Gabriel (1787), William Gunter Lewis (1822-1834), Elizabeth Gunter Lewis (1834-1860), 'E.G. Lewis (late)' (1868-1873).

HANSARD'S MINERAL WATER FACTORY, NO. 12, CROSS STREET
Alfred Hansard (1914)

Owner: John Owen Marsh (1914)

THE ANGEL HOTEL, NO. 15, CROSS STREET
In December 1721, John Scott and his mother, Anne, of the parish of Llantilio Pertholey sold the 'Angel Inn ... in a street or ward ... called Cross Street' to William Dinwoodie of Abergavenny. At that time, the inn was in the occupation of Elizabeth Williams, widow. William Dinwoody was still the

The Angel Hotel in 1845, during the Eisteddfod of the Abergavenny Cymreigyddion.

proprietor in 1736. He was followed by his son, Robert, and then, in 1743, by Samuel Saunders. Samuel Saunders died in October 1778 at the age of eighty, and Charles Hanbury Saunders became sole proprietor. He is still named as the freeholder in *The Universal British Directory* of 1791, which adds that the London coach set off 'every Monday and Friday morning early, to the Bolt-in-Tun, Fleet-street; and returns thence every Sunday and Thursday noon'.

On Thursday 2 May 1793, Sir Richard Colt Hoare, the famous traveller and artist, stayed at the Angel but found the service poor: 'I found a good inn at the Angel, Abergavenny, but bad attendance'.

In August 1797, Revd Richard Warner of Bath had a better experience: 'The clock told nine as we entered Abergavenny; and a walk of eleven miles rendered the excellent breakfast which we met with at the Angel inn particularly grateful'.

By May 1801, the hotel had been entirely rebuilt and was up for sale. The newspaper advertisement announcing the sale reads:

> All that newly erected ... Messuage, called the Angel Inn ... consisting of five Parlours or Sitting Rooms on the Ground floor, one of which is sufficiently large to wine two hundred persons ... two handsome Dining Rooms upon the first floor, with sufficient and neat Bed-chambers ... there are also three good Cellars ... excellent Stabling, a very roomy Chaise Yard for Carriages to stand under Cover; a large and very pleasant Garden.

By 1832, the inn was owned by the Duke of Beaufort. Together with the Greyhound and the George Inn in Frogmore Street, the Angel was one of Abergavenny's three coaching inns. By 1829, with a Mr

Henry Lewis as proprietor, the Angel was a posting inn and office for the mail coaches to London, Milford Haven, Newport, Bristol and Merthyr, and also coaches for Birmingham, Shrewsbury and Aberystwyth. In 1835, *Pigot's Directory for Monmouthshire* lists the following coach services available from the Angel:

To London, the *Royal Mail* (from Milford) ... every forenoon at twenty minutes past eleven – the Nimrod (from Brecon) every morning (Sunday excepted) at half-past nine ... all go through Ragland and Monmouth.

To Brecon, the *Nimrod* (from London) ... every afternoon (Sunday excepted) at a quarter past one.

To Hereford ... a Coach ... every afternoon at four.

To Milford, the *Royal Mail* (from London) ... every afternoon at two; goes through Crickhowell, Brecon, &c.

To Newport, the *Royal Mail* ... every morning at eight; goes through Pont y pool and Caerleon.

Charles Price, grocer, wrote his memoirs of old Abergavenny in 1880 and recollected that, at the time of Waterloo, the coaches:

started from the Angel Hotel, the access to the yard being by means of a passage through the front of the hotel, which now forms the vestibule or hall. This passage was so low that persons sitting upon the coach had to stoop to avoid contact with the top of the arch.

Throughout the nineteenth century, the Angel was used as a venue for a variety of social events and gatherings, especially dances and balls. In the 1820s, it was used as a venue for sales and auctions. In 1825, a Ladies' Bible Society met there, while in 1832 a Grand Dinner was held in celebration of the Reform Act. 1838 saw a fancy dress ball to mark the Abergavenny Cymreigyddion Eisteddfod of that year – the dancing went on until 5 a.m.! In February 1879, the hotel was the venue for the annual general meeting of the Abergavenny Quoits Club ('Wm. K. Kynch, Hon. Sec.'). In December 1848, the *Hereford Journal* carried the following report:

Mr Vaughan Morgan, the spirited young landlord of the Angel Hotel, in this town, upon the occasion of succeeding his late father [Thomas Morgan] in business, gave a housewarming dinner of Thursday se'ennight... The dinner was of the most recherché character, and upwards of one hundred persons procured tickets, out of compliment to the landlord, but did not attend.

By March 1859, the Angel was in the hands of Phillip Morgan, who also ran the Greyhound Hotel and by November 1860 he had also taken over the Angel Coach Office from James Vaughan Morgan (probably a relative of Thomas Vaughan Morgan). The following year, J.J.A. Borlase, the vice-president of the Penzance Natural History and Archaeological Society, noted that: 'The coffee room at the Angel is used as the gentlemen's News Room, and the table in the large bow window was well supplied with papers'.

Phillip Morgan bought the hotel outright from the Duke of Beaufort in October 1872. Phillip Morgan's wife, Mary Anne Morgan, played an increasingly important role in the running of the hotel from 1869 onwards. A programme of renovations was undertaken but, despite these improvements, that year's *Handbook for Travellers in South Wales* carried the stark entry 'Hotel: Angel, bad'.

Phillip Morgan had died by December 1872. Mrs Morgan is described as the hotel's proprietress in 1873. In 1875, she entered into a business partnership with Mr James Harraway, who took out a

The Angel in 1903.

lease on the hotel. In August of the same year, Mrs Morgan announced her retirement to Helston in Cornwall. In 1879, Harraway went bankrupt and Mrs Morgan reclaimed the lease.

The following year, 1880, a new tenant, Mr John Prichard, took over and set about the construction of a brand new billiard room. The builder was Thomas Foster, who went on (in around 1907) to build Fosterville. In November 1883, Prichard bought the Angel outright for the sum of £528 5s 6d. In 1884, J.J. Hissey found the Angel, and its new owner, very much to his taste:

> new people had only just taken possession of the place, and there was consequently a good deal of confusion, but everything was beautifully clean, and we were well entertained in spite of the bustle... The next morning being fine encouraged an early start... The landlord here, too, came to wish us good-day and a prosperous journey. These little attentions, which cost nothing, are very pleasing to the travellers, they are something which cannot be bought and paid for.

In 1891, Mr Hissey returned and describes the hotel as:

> one of those past-time hostelries that has retained its old-fashioned ways and look, and where post horses may be had to this day, also good wine for payment, and in the cosy bar gossip free of charge.

By 1886, John Prichard had added 'An Extensive Ball Room and Suite'. *The Ports of the Bristol Channel*, published in 1893, gives a detailed description of the hotel:

> It is well furnished throughout in the best modern style, the fine drawing-room on the first floor being sumptuously furnished and decorated in ebony and gold; while the ball-room, an apartment of noble proportions, is provided with a balcony for the band, a large reception-room, and three or four ante-rooms. Lovers of indoor games have the use of a capital billiard saloon ... while guests desirous of exercising the 'gentle sport' can have good salmon and trout fishing on the River Usk, Mr Prichard having sufficient private water for seven rods, which are placed at the disposal of visitors... The Angel Hotel is the headquarters of the Abergavenny Golf Club, president, Lord Langattock... Visitors can obtain tickets for five shillings per week.

By 1903, the house was being described as a 'CTC. and Automobile Club Hotel' within easy reach of 'Charming Cycle and Motor Roads with unsurpassed Scenery'. In 1907, to add to the hotel's attractions, John Prichard leased the rights for shooting, fowling, coursing, fishing and sporting across all the farmlands, woods and plantations belonging to Charles Kemys-Tynte in Llanelen and the fishing rights on the west bank of the Usk in the same parish. In the early years of the twentieth century, dancing and ballet lessons were held twice-weekly at the Angel for the pupils of Castle Street School.

By 1937, the hotel was able to offer 'Hot and Cold Water in all Bedrooms'. Until the 1950s, the present rear car park contained stabling for horses. In the past, the Angel was obviously a place where the world was often set to rights. In his memoir, Richard Merton Jones regrets that 'we no longer see the City Fathers assembling nightly in the corner of the Angel Bar to settle the events of the world'.

Publicans: Elizabeth Williams (1721), William Dinwoody (1736), Samuel Saunders (1743-1778), Charles Hanbury Saunders (1778-1791), Josiah Crutchley (1811), Henry Lewis (1822-1823), Elizabeth Lewis (1829-1835), Charles Barrett (1839), Thomas Morgan (1840-1847), Thomas Vaughan Morgan (1848-1853), Phillip Morgan (March 1859-1872), Mrs Mary Anne Morgan (1873-1875), James Harraway (1875-1879), John Prichard (1880-1906), Hubert Beynon Stocken (1910-1914), James Thomas (1920), Trust Houses Ltd (1923).

Changing times and changing modes of transport - the Angel, c. 1904. By this time, a garage had been added to the hotel's stables.

Owners (when known): John Scott and Anne Scott (1721), William Dinwoody (1721-1736), Charles Hanbury Saunders (1791), Duke of Beaufort (1832-October 1872), Phillip Morgan (October-December 1872), Mary Anne Morgan (1873-1883), John Prichard (1883), Hubert Beynon Stocken (1914), Trusthouse Forte (1923).

THE SWAN HOTEL, NO. 33, CROSS STREET
(also known as the New Swan or the Lower Swan)

Reference is made in a document of 1680 to Henry Baker as the owner of the Swan, though whether this refers to the White Swan, the Black Swan or the Swan Hotel is not clear.

The earliest record of the New Swan Hotel dates to 14 January 1829, when a Society of Tradesmen and Gentlemen Farmers was formed there. In April 1829, the men were followed by a Friendly Society of Women, and Benjamin Fox was landlord. The St Mary's parish registers record the marriage of 'Benjamin Fox, victualler' to his first wife, Elizabeth Price, in September 1824 and to his second, Sarah Davies, in November 1825.

The hotel had recently been rebuilt and had become known as the New Swan or Lower Swan to differentiate it from the White Swan at the top of Cross Street. In 1880, 'an Abergavenny Octogenarian' recorded his memories of the place before it was rebuilt:

a small two-storeyed building to which entrance was obtained by a descent of two steps, the street being then at that place several feet higher than it is at present. The only way out of the town was through lower Mill-street, and out at Pen y Cawse, and the site of the road from the Swan by the Bridge Inn was occupied by fields and gardens. There was a small yard behind the Swan where the stage waggons put up ... and they brought shop goods twice or thrice a week from Caerleon, which was a place of some importance in those days.

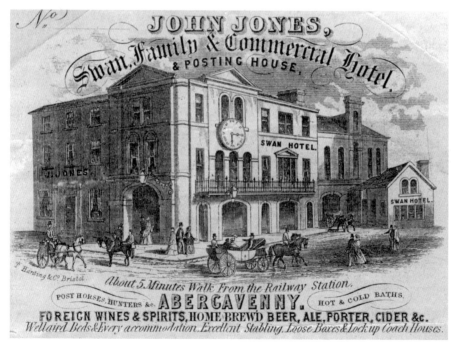

The Swan Hotel in 1884.

In September 1832, the women's friendly society which had used the Swan as its headquarters moved to the Unicorn. In 1852, the place is described as a 'Family and Commercial Inn and Posting House'. In May 1875, John Goodwin sold the hotel to Henry Wibberley. In 1884, the hotel advertised 'Foreign Wines and Spirits, Home Brew'd Beer, Ale, Porter, Cider &c. Wellaird Beds'. It was also listed as the general headquarters of the Cyclists' Touring Club. In January 1899, the hotel was put up for sale and is described in the particulars as a:

> Family, Commercial & Agricultural Hotel & Posting House... On the Ground Floor: Handsome Entrance Hall, paved with encaustic tiles, Commercial Room, Smoking Room, Market Room, Bar... Upstairs: Large Coffee Room ... with French Windows opening on Balcony... capital specially-designed Ball Room, 75 feet by 30 feet, with Band Orchestra, and separate entrance Stair-case from outside.

During the Second World War, American troops were stationed in Abergavenny. Peter Coleman recollected their effect on the Swan in *Abergavenny in the Twentieth Century*:

> They took over the Swan Hotel as their headquarters. The Swan Hotel was twice the size it is now. Vehicles would pull up under the veranda and spill out their passengers, and at the rear of the Swan reaching out towards Priory Lane was a great dance hall, and there were so many Americans using the place that they decided to shore it up with special pillars underneath. This really became the centre of activity for the town. At the end of the war the Americans left, compensation was paid to the owners and the place was sold and the new people decided to remove these pillars and the ballroom and rooms above it collapsed into a heap of rubble.

The Swan Hotel in the early years of the twentieth century. The brick building on the left behind the gas lamp is the Tanner's Arms in Mill Street.

Publicans: Benjamin Fox (1824-1830), John Dix (1835-1844), John Goodwin (1850-1877), William Gregory Chappell (1876-1877), John Jones (1879-1891), Francis John Lawrence (1895), Thomas Sikes (1899), Philip Lawrence Lloyd (1901-1906), Walter Fancourt, manager (1910-1912), William Henry Whitehead (1914-1921), Arthur Holmes (1923-1930), W.J. Davies (1930-1931), F. Norman Groom (1933-1934), Mrs P.L. Lloyd (1937), Ellen Lloyd (1938-1939).
Owners (when known): Henry Baker (1680), Richard James (1839-1840), John Goodwin (1850-May 1875), Philip L. Lloyd (1914), Ellen Lloyd (1938-1939).

THE CARDIFF ARMS, NO. 39, CROSS STREET
(formerly the Parrot Inn)
Originally built by the wealthy Gunter family as a town residence in the sixteenth century, these premises were run as a beerhouse from 1856 onwards. The earliest known publican was Robert Thomas and, by 1864, the pub was known as the Parrot Inn. In 1897, the name was changed to the Cardiff Arms.

By May 1898, the pub was owned by Mrs Mary Phillips who conveyed it to Edwin Arthur Johnson (on 5 May) who, in turn, sold it (on 9 May!) to John Thompson Jenkins and George Edwards of Tredegar, brewers, for £1,500. The conveyance dated 5 May describes the pub as being in the occupation of Samuel Henry Facey, the local brewer (*see* the White Swan and Market Street).

The last landlord, William Homer, went bankrupt in 1907 and, in the November of the same year, the Hereford and Tredegar Brewery sold the building to Thomas Smith Foster, the builder of Fosterville, with a view to conversion into shops and residential premises. It was during the conversion that the secret Catholic chapel dating from the 1670s was discovered in the loft, complete with the mural that acted as an altarpiece. This is now on display in the museum.

Publicans: Robert Thomas (1856-1858), ? Probert (1860), John Howells (1864), William Powell (January 1864-December 1869), William Powell (December 1870), Mrs Elizabeth Powell (1871), James Randall (July 1872-1879), Robert Gardner (1884), Arthur Davies (1891-1895), Samuel Henry Facey (5 May 1898), John Jenkins and George Edwards (9 May 1898), David James (1901), William Homer and Edward Francis (1906-1907).
Owners (when known): Mary Thomas (1856-1860), Robert Thomas (1864-February 1867), John Watkins (February 1867-1873), Mrs Mary Phillips (1898), Edwin Arthur Johnson (1898), John Jenkins and George Edwards, brewers (1898), Hereford and Tredegar Brewery (1907).

THE COACH AND HORSES, NO. 41, CROSS STREET
(formerly the Sun Inn)
The Sun was certainly in existence in 1787, when William Davies was the landlord. In 1794, he was paid £7 6s compensation by the Abergavenny Improvement Commissioners for the loss of part of his premises when the medieval South Gate of the town was demolished for road widening. By 1817, William Davies had died – a document dated 14 June of that year names his son, William Davies, yeoman, and widow, Mary, as joint owners of 'The Sun with brew house stable and yard'.

In March 1823, a 'Society of Tradesmen and others' was founded at the pub. On 22 November 1833, the Sun was the venue for the inaugural meeting of Cymdeithas Cymreigyddion y Fenni, the Abergavenny Cymreigyddion Society, and for several years their annual eisteddfod (which eventually developed into the National Eisteddfod) was held there. In the Cymreigyddion minutes, John Michael, the landlord at the time, is styled 'Ioan Mitchell' in good Welsh fashion. On 19 October 1837, the

The Sun Inn on market day, c. 1923.

society organised an 'ordinary' (a public meal at a fixed time and price) here at four o'clock for visitors to their fourth eisteddfod. The previous day, it had been held at the George Inn in Frogmore Street.

In December 1839, the pub was home to the Friendly Club, with the publican, John Michael, as treasurer. In 1862, the landlord, William Cook, also doubled as the Abergavenny agent for Proctor's Artificial Manure! In June 1903, the pub was taken over by Daniel Delafield, whose father ran Delafield's Brewery behind the King's Arms.

A Mr and Mrs Delaney ran the pub for many years during the 1960s and 1970s. The pub was renamed the Coach and Horses in 1973.

Publicans: William Davies (1787-1817), John Michael (1822-1850), William Rowley (May 1850 -1858), William Cook (1859-1876, 'Mrs Cooke' is listed in the Water Rate Book of 1868), Abraham Watkins (1884), Mrs Mary Watkins (1891-1901), Daniel Delafield (1903-1906), Thomas Brown (1910), Thomas Jones (1912-1914), John H. Watkins (1923), Mrs Sarah Denner (1926), William Denner (1927-1939).
Owners (when known): William Davies (1787-died 1817), William Davies and Mary Davies (1817), Michael Phillips (1839-June 1851), Mr Jones (July 1851-1853), Mrs Jones (1859-1860), Thomas Jones (1864), William Jones (1868), Thomas Jones (1872), J.W. Harvey (1873), Richard Baker Gabb (May 1914), Charles Edwards Brewery Ltd (June 1914-1939).

THE CROWN INN, NO. 45, CROSS STREET

The first recorded landlord of the Crown Inn is a certain 'Mr Lewellin' in 1787. In 1791, Abraham Llewellin is listed as the publican and freeholder. By 1802, he had been succeeded by Charles Fuller.

On 8 September in that year, the Abergavenny Improvement Commissioners (the forerunners of the Borough Council) appointed him 'Scavenger for one year from this day ... to sweep, cleanse and remove for his own use all ashes, rubbish, dung, dunghills, dirt and filth ... in the streets'.

It is obvious that the responsibilities of his new post were too much for Mr Fuller, for by 3 December, he was declining to do the job and Thomas Evans of the King's Head Inn was appointed to replace him. As William Price recollected in 1880, the pub seems to have had a very enterprising landlord at around the time of Waterloo:

> The London mail [coach] arrived every evening at half-past eight, and returned from Milford and Carmarthen at four o'clock the next morning ... the landlord of the Crown Inn, Cross-street, used to be up by three o'clock in the morning in time for the arrival of the coach, and to many a cold, drenched outside traveller the light which flickered in the little window of that hostelry, looking up Cross-street, afforded a welcome sight, indicating as it did that he had reached another stage of his journey, and telling him of warmth and creature comforts that were awaiting him within.

In August 1841, the publican, John Horton, registered as the treasurer of the Society of Gentlemen and Tradesmen held at his inn. By December 1846, the pub had been taken over by George Dawkins.

By July 1872, William Cook, the landlord of the Sun Inn, had bought the freehold on the Crown, though the pub was run by Mary Ann Proverbs. In September 1907, the pub was leased to Louis John Daley by the then owner, Alfred Cooke, at the princely yearly rent of £35. The pub burned down in 1930 and was replaced by the office for Moon's Garage, which stood opposite. By 1939, it was known as the Jubilee Garage.

Publicans: Mr Lewellin (1787), Abraham Llewellin (1791), Charles Fuller (1802), James Bennett (1822-1823), James Cole (1830-1835), William Davies (1839-1840), John Horton (August 1841-1844), George Dawkins (December 1846-1850), William White Wheeler (1851-1852), Henry W. Hodder (1853), Robert Smith (1858-1860), Thomas Watkins (1862), Thomas Jones (1862-1865), S. Munkley (1868), John Price (1871), Mrs Mary Ann Proverbs (1873-1875), William Cook and Mary Ann Proverbs (1877), Mrs Mary Ann Proverbs (1884), Frederick Meredith (1891), William Casey (1895), Joseph Williams (1901), Albert Matthews (1906), Louis John Daley (1907), Edward Peake (1910-1914), Griffith Williams (1914), Edward Edwards (1920), Allen Edward Burgess (1923), John Henry Watkins (19261931).

Owners (when known): Abraham Llewellin (1791), John Lewis (1839-1840), William Price (1850), William White Wheeler (1851), Wheeler and Davies (1853), George Window (1859-1868), William Cook (July 1872-1880), Alfred Cooke (1907-1914).

THE DUKE OF WELLINGTON INN, NO 46, CROSS STREET
(formerly the Harp)

This hostelry was originally known as the Harp. It is first mentioned in 1787 when a Mr Mallowny was the landlord. In 1791, Ann Malony is recorded as the publican and freeholder. John Burl Mallowney died in 1814 and it is possible that the name changed then or shortly after – possibly after the Battle of Waterloo. It was certainly known as the Duke of Wellington by 1822. In 1852, the publican, Joseph Cole, is described as a 'victualler, licensed to sell horses'.

In October 1883, John Powell, formerly of the Blorenge Inn on the Monmouth Road, took out a seven-year lease on the premises from the then owner and innkeeper, William Cupid Warr, for an annual rent of £35 'except the Butcher's Shop adjoining on the south side ... and the bedrooms over the same'. By that time, it was known simply as the Wellington Inn. In March 1888, John Powell leased the premises in turn to Matthew Gooden of Gilwern, until October 1890.

In 1891, the pub was advertised as having sufficient stabling for forty horses and 'ample accommodation for visitors'. In 1947, the site was sold to Lewis' Electrical Co., and was taken over by Peter Dominic as an off-licence in 1962.

Publicans: John Burl Mallowney (1787–died 1814; Ann Malony listed in 1791), Thomas Roberts (1822), Daniel Jones (1830), John Horton (1835-1840), Joseph Cole (1842-1853), William Knight (1858-1864), John Child (1865), William Cupid Warr (1868-1883), John Powell (1883-1888), Matthew Gooden (1888-1890), Edward Pottinger (1891), John David Williams (1895-1901), Henry H. Bates (1906-1912), Clement Morgan Barber (1914), Charles Pugh (1920), George Maggs (1923), John Evans Davies (1926-1931), Mrs Emmeline Miller (1934), William Frederick Higman (1937-1939).
Owners (when known): Ann Malony (1791), F.H. Williams (1839-1864), William Cupid Warr (1868-1884), George Powell (1914-1938).

THE GREAT GEORGE, NO. 49, CROSS STREET
(formerly the Bellamy Wine Vaults)
Between 1690 and 1707, the site was occupied by the Independent Congregationalist Meeting House, which subsequently moved to its present site in Castle Street. Acquired by Mr W.E. Bellamy in 1775, the premises opened under the name of the Bellamy Wine Vaults. The Bellamy family was to run the business for 100 years.

In 1840, John Bellamy was a juror in the trial of John Frost, one of the leaders of the Chartist Uprising of November 1839. He died in April 1841. By 1856, the premises had been improved by the

The former Duke of Wellington, on the extreme right, c. 1950.

addition of billiard rooms and reading rooms and the *Abergavenny Trade Directory* for 1858 records that Mr William Bellamy 'resided in the newly converted Castle, a picturesque and secluded retreat'. The Street and Water Rate Book of 1868 lists the Vaults as vacant but by 1871 they were open for business again under the management of Benjamin Nicholls.

The business was taken over by Charles Tucker in 1875. In *The Ports of the Bristol Channel*, published in 1893, the business is described in some detail:

> The retail department faces into Cross Street...The wholesale branch is in Monk Street ... and the firm hold a very large bonded stock at their stores under the market ... of the most noted vintages, including rich crusted port, pale and golden sherry, Clicquot's, Moet's, Mumm's, and Giesler's champagnes, and claret and hock of various kinds, as well as splendid supplies of brandy, whisky, rum, and a fine selection of foreign liqueurs and English cordials ... also agents for the Lorne whisky and for Stewart's well-known whisky, Cream of the Barley; also the noted Canadian whisky, as well as for the celebrated Alton Court Brewery, Bass's and Salt's ales, and Guinness's stout ... also local representatives of the London and Norwich Insurance Company, and the Phoenix Fire Office.

An advert in the *Abergavenny Chronicle* of 12 April 1895 names Alfred Jenkins as the landlord. By 1905, the premises were known as the George. In that year, Alfred Jenkins organised the special luncheon in the Town Hall to mark the visit to the town of Lord Roberts of Kandahar and was granted a special licence from 12 noon to 4 p.m. for the purpose. For a brief period in May and June 1914, the pub reverted to the name of the Wine Vaults.

Publicans: W.E. Bellamy (1775), John Bellamy (1822-died 1841, still listed 1842-1844), Bellamy and Son (1850), Mrs Eliza Bellamy (June 1851), Eliza Bellamy and Son (July 1851), John Massey Bellamy (1852), William E. Bellamy (1853-1860), S. M. Bellamy (1862), Mrs Bellamy (1864), Mrs P.W. Bellamy (1865-1868), Benjamin Nicholls, for Bellamy & Co. (1871), J.M. Bellamy (1872), Mrs Bellamy (1873), Bellamy & Co. (1875, 1877), Charles Tucker (1875-1889), Charles Tucker and Son (1889-1893), Alfred Jenkins (1895-1910), Francis Albert McGraith (1914) with Mrs Mary A. Jones (1920), A. Lewis (1923), Mrs Sarah Jane Lewis (1926-1931), G. Griffiths (1934), William J. Harris (1937), Albert Bailey (1938), F. Bailey (1939).
Owners (when known): Revd R.W.P. Davies (1834-1873), Hereford and Tredegar Brewery Co. (1914-1939).

THE QUEEN'S HEAD, NO. 50, CROSS STREET
(formerly the Old George Inn)
The earliest record of the Old George Inn dates back to a document dated 26 July 1732, which mentions 'the Old George, late in the tenure of John Somersett, Esq.' In March 1733, the pub was leased by John John of 'Kevendoyglod' (i.e. Cefndwyglwyd near Llanvapley) to Roger Yarnold, 'glasier and plumer' and is described as standing in Old George Street. This name obviously refers to the stretch of road from the Cross Street junction to the old town gate which stood next to where Laburnum Cottage now stands.

An indenture dated 15 November 1810 describes the 'dwelling house heretofore called the Old George' as 'the property of ... Joseph Harrison and in the holding of John Rees, Maltster'.

A mortgage of 21 November 1815, which names 'Morgan Walbeoff, yeoman and William Hiley of Llanwenarth, gent., and Mary Hiley of Caerleon, widow' as the owners, describes the pub as a messuage 'called Old George afterward the Queen's Head with malt house, stable and additional buildings built by Roger Yarnold'. By 1822, the premises were being run as a baker's shop by Philip Pyefinch.

By 1862, the house had become a draper's shop, though the malthouse continued in operation and was eventually taken over by Samuel Trotter, who certainly ran it as a brewery from 1842 (listed as Williams & Trotter until 1844) to 1862 (*see* the Royal Victoria Brewery). The building was finally demolished in 1932 in order to widen Monk Street.

Publicans: John Somersett (pre-1732), Roger Yarnold (1733), Mrs Evans (1800), John Rees (November 1810).
Owners (when known): Robert Harries (pre-1732), John Jones 'of Panty Goytre' (1732), John John (1733), Joseph Harrison (November 1810), Morgan Walbeoff, William Hiley and Mary Hiley (1815).

THE PORTER STORES, NO. 55, CROSS STREET
(also known as the Vaults, the Ale and Porter Stores or the Spirit Vaults)
This pub is first recorded as the Vaults in 1850, under the management of Ebenezer Michael. It is still referred to as the Vaults in 1858 but then seems to have closed for a brief period, as the Poor Rate Book for 1859 lists it only as a house and shop. However, by 1860 it was back in business and renamed the Porter Stores, with John Warwick as landlord. In 1862, it is referred to as the Spirit Vaults. By 1865, the landlord was John Poole and the pub was known as the Ale and Porter Stores. By 1868, the owner was George Window (who also owned the Crown Inn) but the pub was still run by John Poole and known once more as the Porter Stores. The last known landlord was William Phillips in 1897, when the pub was pulled down to make way for what is now Lloyd's Bank.

Publicans: Ebenezer Michael (1850-1858), John Warwick (1860-1862), John Poole (1865-1884), Elizabeth Speers (1887), William Phillips (1891-1897).
Owners (when known): Ebenezer Michael (1853), John Warwick (1860-1862), George Window (1868), Mrs Window (1873).

THE KING'S HEAD, NO. 60, CROSS STREET
The earliest record of the King's Head dates back to 1689, in the will of the landlord, Edward Lewis, who died in that year.

On 16 October 1800, the inn was put up for sale by Hanbury Williams of Coldbrook 'by Mr Croft at 2 p.m. at the Greyhound Inn', though we do not know who bought it.

From 1797 to 1827, the Abergavenny Improvement Commissioners met at the pub, and on 3 December 1802 the landlord, Mr Thomas Evans, was officially appointed by them as the Town Scavenger in place of Mr Charles Fuller, landlord of the Crown Inn, who had refused to do the job. In 1803, the pub's long room was used for the meetings of the Abergavenny Loyal Volunteer Infantry. This fine body of men had been formed during the Napoleonic Wars to resist the threat of a possible French invasion. The Turnpike Trust also met here in 1810. Writing in around 1880, William Price recollected that in the period around 1817, the Abergavenny Improvement Commissioners met at the King's Head, while the magistrates sat at the London Apprentice in Monk Street.

In 1836, the then proprietor, William Watkins, was granted permission by the Abergavenny Improvement Commissioners to move the medieval arch, which is still a feature of the building, to its present position and to build the current frontage. A glimpse of the old frontage can just be seen on an 1826 print of the marketplace and this seems to show a late seventeenth-century building with a central gable.

By July 1837, when the Old Bull Friendly Society moved to the King's Head, the landlord was James Cole. In 1839, he served as a juror in the trial for treason of the leaders of the Chartist Uprising at Newport. The Rate Book for 1840, dated 12 June, lists him as the 'Late James Cole' and by 23 September the pub had been taken over by Charles Jennings, who also took over as treasurer of the Old King's Head Friendly Society. In September 1850, the men were joined by a Women's Benefit Society, which had moved up from the Unicorn in Mill Street – it was still at the King's Head in February 1852. In May 1852, Mary Jennings registered herself as the treasurer of both these societies, probably when she took over management of the pub. By May 1854, Joseph Brown had moved to the King's Head from the King's Arms and both societies were still flourishing. However, in December 1863, one of them moved to the Old Duke in Castle Street.

By 1871, the business had passed to Peter Edwin Wynn, described in 1874 as an 'Importer of Wines and Spirit'. He also acted as the agent for Alsopp's Ales and Guinness's Stout. He had started his career as the manager of Bellamy's Wine Vaults (*see* the Great George) and is listed there in 1865.

Until the late 1920s, the stables at the rear of the premises were used on market days to accommodate around forty horses, with their carts packed tightly across Cross Street.

The King's Head and the Town Hall in the 1960s.

Publicans: Edward Lewis (1689), Mr Warner (1787), William Warner (1791), Thomas Evans (1802), Margaret Evans (1811), James Jones (1822), Thomas Evans (1830), Elizabeth Evans (1835), William Watkins (1836), James Cole (1837-died by June 1840), Charles Jennings (September 1840-May 1852), Mary Jennings (May 1852-1853), Joseph Brown (May 1854-1859), ? Maddox (1860), James Alden (1862-1865), ? Prosser (1868), Peter Edwin Wynn (1871-1877), John Howe (1880-1891), William Williams (1895), Daniel Christmas Davies (1901), Henry Lewis (1906), David Powell (1910-1912), Mrs Alice C. Powell (May 1914-1934), Arthur Edgar Tutt (1937-1939).

Owners (when known): Hanbury Williams (1800), James Cole (1839-1840), William Watkins (1836-1868), William Williams Jnr (1872), William Williams (1873), Charles Berry Williams (1880), Arnold Perett & Co. Brewery Ltd (1914-1938).

THE DOG AND BULL AND THE PLUME OF FEATHERS, ON THE SITE OF THE PRESENT TOWN HALL

In 1794, John Nash, later the architect of the Brighton Pavilion, was commissioned by the Abergavenny Improvement Commissioners to design a new market hall. In order to construct the new building (on the site of the present Town Hall) two taverns and several dwelling houses had to be demolished. The taverns were the Plume of Feathers, with John Morgan as landlord, and the Dog and Bull, run by Mary Price, both first recorded in 1787. In compensation for their loss, Mary Price received £262 10s 0d, while Charles Herbert, ironmonger, the owner of the Plume was awarded £315.

The name Dog and Bull refers to the once-popular sport of bull-baiting, where dogs, usually bulldogs or bull mastiffs, were set to attack bulls. Bull-baiting was very popular in Abergavenny until the mid-nineteenth century but as early as 1794 the Improvement Commissioners decided to take firm action to suppress it:

> It having been reported to the Commissioners that certain innkeepers within the town, frequently harboured bulls in their stables and outbuildings for the purpose of having them baited in defiance of the law and good order, we, therefore, do earnestly recommend it to the magistrates not to continue the license of those persons who shall be found hereafter so offending.

In the same year, the Commissioners paid for the defence of Thomas Leonard and William Price at the Quarter Sessions on a charge of assault against John Vaughan who was 'discovered by them baiting and chasing a bull in the town in the night-time of the 27th of September, 1794'. The Commissioners also paid Mr William Lewis of The Brooks the sum of £2 8s, that being 'the expense incurred by him for indicting several persons for taking his bull from his grounds and baiting it in the streets of the town'. No wonder that the local nickname for people from the town was Abergavenny Bulldogs!

Publicans: Dog and Bull: Mr Bowler (1787), ? Davies (1791), Mary Price (1794). Plume of Feathers: William Rogers (1787-1791), John Morgan (1794).

Owners (when known): Dog and Bull: Mary Price (1794). Plume of Feathers: Charles Herbert (1794).

THE BLUE BOAR

Although a pub by the name of the Boar is recorded in Abergavenny as early as 1730, it is not known whether this is the same house as that 'commonly known by the name of the blue boar in Cross Street', which is first recorded in June 1741. It belonged to the parish of Temple in the city of Bristol and, on 19 June in that year, Mr John Bevan, churchwarden, leased the pub to Benjamin Moses for the sum of

£10 a year. It seems that Mr Moses did not take to the pub trade, for in January 1742 he gave notice that he intended to quit the possession of the pub on 25 March and that the churchwarden would then be at liberty to 'provide another tenant for the said'.

The pub appears to have been in a very sorry state because on 26 May 1743, William Yarnold, a local builder, submitted a bill for extensive repairs that came to the princely sum of £42 2s. This included the cost of altering the brewhouse to a stable, and 12s for a new pub sign! In May 1749, the pub was leased to Susannah Nicholas, widow, for the sum of £40 and that is the last mention of the Blue Boar.

Publicans: Benjamin Moses (June 1741-March 1742), Susannah Nicholas (1749).
Owners (when known): the vicar and churchwardens of the parish of Temple in the city of Bristol (1741-1749).

BEERHOUSES (LOCATIONS UNKNOWN)
Edward Probert (1862), possibly at the Parrot Inn.

FLANNEL STREET

THE HEN AND CHICKENS, NO. 7, FLANNEL STREET

Although the history of the building dates back at least to the seventeenth century, the first recorded publican of the Hen and Chickens was Rachel Cadogan in 1822. In 1834, Wood's map of Abergavenny clearly shows the pub with a large yard at the rear opening on to St John's Street. Until the establishment of the cattle market in Lion Street in 1867, the town's poultry market was held in Chicken Street and St John's Street, hence the name Hen and Chickens!

Between 1864 and 1873, the Hen and Chickens was owned by William Trew. He had been the publican of the Three Tuns in Mill Street, the Bridgend Inn on the Monmouth Road and the Clarence Inn in Castle Street. In 1851, William had married Elizabeth Herbert, the owner of the London Apprentice in Monk Street and so had added that pub to his licensed empire. He was also a butcher!

In 1875, the house was known as the Hen and Chickens Inn and Dining Rooms. On a billhead dated 4 March 1900, it is described as the Hen and Chickens Hotel and Restaurant and the proprietor named as T.T. Jones. In that same year, the 'Chicks' was taken over by Annie Williams, whose licences for the years 1900-1902 are preserved in the museum. In May 1901, Mrs Williams submitted a tender for catering for a luncheon in honour of the Abergavenny volunteers returning from the Boer War:

> I can provide First Class Luncheon at 1/6 per head consisting of Roast Lamb, Mint Sauce, Roast Veal, Beef or Mutton, Bread, Cheese & Salad, Cucumber, & Pastry, Beers & Stouts of the Best qualities, Worthingtons Burton-on-Tent, Yorath & Sons Newport, Scotch Whiskies – Dewars, Irish do.- Thomsons, Brandy – Martells, Gin & Rum.

Unfortunately for Mrs Williams, the contract went to the Greyhound Hotel. In 1911, the well-known Anglo-Welsh poet, W.H. Davies, stayed at the pub. He evidently enjoyed his stay because, by dawn, he was 'just sober enough to stop himself from murdering his coat and cap on the bed-post with a swordstick'.

Publicans: Rachel Cadogan (1822-1830), Elizabeth Havard (1835), William Liles (1840), James Chamberlain (1842-1844), Paulina Gwatkin (1850-1860), Walter Jones (1862-1865; died 19 December

The Hen and Chickens, prior to the demolition of the rest of Flannel Street in 1957.

1866, aged sixty, and is buried at Oldcastle church), Mrs Jones (1868), Mrs Paulina Jones (1871-July 1872), T. Jones (1873), Thomas Theophilus Jones (1875-1900), Mrs Annie Williams (1900-1902), Frederick Williams (1906-1910), Ernest Williams (1912-1920), Albert Bailey (1923), Frank Gough (1926), William Alfred Brinsdon (1934-1937), L.T.G. Berrington (1937-1938), H. Berrington (1939). *Owners* (when known): Rachel Cadogan (1839), William Liles (1840), Mr Kyrwood (1850), Mrs Kyrwood (1851), 'late R. Kerwood' (1853), William Havard (1856-1860), William Trew (1864-1868), Theophilus Jones (July 1972), William Trew (1873), Theophilus Jones (1880), Ernest Williams (1914), L.T.G. Berrington (1938).

THE OLD BARLEY MOW, NO. 8, FLANNEL STREET
Again, the history of this building stretched back to the seventeenth or possibly the sixteenth century. It was run as an eating-house by Mrs Elizabeth Liles from 1875 onwards and is first recorded as a beerhouse, run by William Daniel Bowles, in 1884. Sometime between 1910 and 1912, it became known as the Old Barley Mow. In 1923, the premises were being run as dining rooms by Harry Harden and are listed as Ye Old Barley Mow Restaurant. The building was demolished in 1958.

Publicans: William Daniel Bowles (1884), Thomas Lewis (1891), James Ball (1901), William John Morgan (1906-1912), Henry Harden (1914).
Owners (when known): ? Shaw (1914).

The Old Barley Mow in the mid-1950s.

THE JOHN BULL, BUTCHERS' ROW

This pub started out as a beerhouse and is first recorded in 1835, with Richard Proudley as the licensee. In fact, it is only listed as the John Bull once, in 1839. By that time, a Sarah Carver was running the pub, though Richard Proudley still owned the property. It is listed as being in Butchers' Row. We do not know where the pub stood but we do know that Sarah Carver was still there in 1850. By 1852, she was running the business as an eating-house.

Publicans: Richard Proudley (1835), Sarah Carver (1839-1850).
Owners (when known): Richard Proudley (1839-1840), John Mason (1850).

BEERHOUSES

No. 18, Flannel Street, listed only once, in 1865.

Publicans: William Pritchard (1865).

No. 21, Flannel Street

This beerhouse is first recorded in 1858. In 1862, the publican, William Liles, is described as being the proprietor of an eating-house and beer retailer. By 1871, the premises were being run purely as dining rooms, though still by Mrs Liles. By 1875, she had moved the business to No. 8, Flannel Street (*see* the Old Barley Mow).

Publicans: William Liles (1858–1865), Mrs Liles (1868).

Owners (when known): Richard Shaw (1868).

At various times, other beer retailers are listed in Flannel Street, though it is not known where their houses stood. They are William Powell (1858) and Mrs Caroline Young (1895).

FROGMORE STREET

THE GOLDEN LION, NO. 6, FROGMORE STREET

(later known as the Sugarloaf)

The Golden Lion gave its name to Lion Street and, before its closure, was the oldest recorded pub in Abergavenny. At the Public Record Office in London, the records of the Court of Star Chamber for the year 1591 to 1592 include a complaint brought by William Lloyd against William Roger, Matthew Wroth, John, William and Matthew David Nicholas and William Thomas. It states that:

> The complainant kept a tavern in the town with a lion and a bush as its sign, but the defendants beat down the sign and assaulted the complainant at Abergavenny on his arrival from London.

Unfortunately for William Lloyd, not only was Matthew Wroth a wealthy man (his grandfather had left him a tan-house in Mill Street in 1586) but he was the son of John Wroth, one of the local magistrates. So, when William Lloyd tried to obtain justice locally, the magistrates found him guilty of affray! As a result, William Lloyd brought more charges in the Court of Star Chamber, this time against John Wroth and William Wolf, namely:

> corruption of justice at the Law Day there to prevent the complainant from bringing an action in Quarter Sessions; corrupt finding of the complainant guilty of an affray.

In January 1662, Thomas William Watkins sold the inn to John William Parry of Pen-y-Clawdd who gave it over to the use of Roger Scudamore. In March 1663, John Parry the elder of Pen-y-Clawdd sold it in turn to James James and the pub is described as then being in the occupation of Jenkin Jones and 'late' in that of Charles Price.

In March 1667, James James leased the Lion to Edward and Elizabeth Rumsey and a full inventory was made of the fixtures and fittings. The inventory lists all the rooms in the house – 'the Barre', the old parlour, the new parlour, the buttery, the gallery, the 'Dineing Roome' (which contained 'one long shuffle board Table, one square table, one potte cupboarde, one great Chest, with formes and wainscott Rownd'), the 'Sheriffes Chamber', the kitchen (which had a 'Cubbe for Powltrie'), the beer cellar, wine cellar, brewhouse, stables and the privy.

The Lion could obviously accommodate a great many paying guests, as the inventory also lists no less than eight 'bedsteedes'(one of which was 'nexte the Privy'!), three 'trundle beddes' (small beds on wheels which could be pushed under a larger bed when not in use) and one 'halfe bedsteede'. In addition, there were 'Seavan ffeather beds, five Bowlsters & one pillow weighing sixe hundred and three Pounds' and 'one fflocke bedde weighing sixtie two pounds'.

A document dated October 1676 states that the 'Golden Lyon' was in the possession of James James the elder, who leased it for one year for the sum of 5s to William Allen, who was to marry his granddaughter, Bridget.

In 1678, Father David Lewis, the Catholic priest arrested for saying Mass at various places (including the secret chapel at the Gunter Mansion in Cross Street) was brought to the Golden Lion for questioning by John Arnold of Llanfihangel Court, the local MP. David Lewis was hanged at Usk on 27 August 1679. He is now a saint of the Roman Catholic Church.

In 1689, an enquiry was held by Charles Price, the sheriff of the county (who presumably stayed in the 'Sheriffes Chamber') at 'the Dwellinghouse of John Greeneheugh ... inn holder commonly called the Golden Lyon' as to whether a new market at Pontypool would be to 'the damage or prejudice' of the Crown or others. The twelve-man jury found that it would not and Pontypool got its market. By December 1732, the pub had been rebuilt and was being advertised in the *Glocester Journal* (5 December) to be let:

> The Ancient Lyon Inn ... containing five rooms on the first floor, seven on the second and third floors each, also two cellars, one Brewhouse, two Stables, a large Garden and Backside and three pieces of Meadow ground thereunto adjoining... It stands convenient for Travellers to and from Brecon, Carmarthen and North-Wales

A map of 1760 shows a 'Fives Court' in the tavern yard and the 'Pig Market' on the adjoining plot in Lion Street. For many years, horse sales were held in the pub yard as well. In 1787, the publican is named as a Mr Jones and in 1791 Jenkin Jones is listed as both victualler and freeholder of the Golden Lion. A later document states that on Christmas Day 1795, Jenkin Jones took out a 21-year lease on 4 acres of meadowland behind the pub known as Lion Fields. By that time, he also owned the Black Swan.

In August 1803, the house was put up for sale and was described as 'well situated for Business' and as being in the occupation of Thomas Morgan. Also included in the sale were the Lion Fields and the

The Golden Lion in 1911.

Lamb Inn opposite. The Lion was bought by 'William Jones of Abergavenny, gent.' for £1,020 and the property actually changed hands on 1 February 1804. The deed recording the sale records that the pub was occupied by 'Jenkins Jones, Mrs Jenkin Jones and Thomas Morgan, victualler, respectively'.

In his will, dated 31 January 1828, Thomas Jones of Abergavenny left 'the King David with stables, and the Golden Lion and land known as the old fish pond situated near Frogmore St ... to Thomas Jones on attaining the age of 21'.

On 20 November 1828, the inaugural meeting of the Abergavenny Union Society (a friendly society for tradesmen) was held at the inn. The society was still active in 1830. In 1839, the publican, William Crump, served as a juror at the trial of the leaders of the Chartist Uprising. By 1840, a coach was sent daily to meet the Bristol to Newport packet boat across the Severn. In 1865, the pub is described as the Golden Lion Agricultural and Commercial Inn.

A document of 1873 lists the property in Abergavenny inherited by Elizabeth Latham as heir of Thomas Jones, Coldbrook, including the 'Golden Lion Hotel, Frogmore Street, Abergavenny, formerly Piscodlin Field'. She was also the owner of the King David. Elizabeth Latham was certainly dead by April 1878.

In August 1897, the Golden Lion, together with the King David, was offered up for sale by auction. The sale particulars describe the hotel as 'in the occupation of Mr Charles Knight ... and is Particularly Celebrated for its Home Brewed Ale'.

The premises had been held by Charles Knight under a 21-year repairing lease since 1 April 1883, at a rent of £78 per annum.

In 1903, the stableyard of the inn was the scene of a contretemps that was fully reported in the *Abergavenny Chronicle* of 8 May, under the headline 'Troublesome':

> W----- P-----, Cross Ash, farmer, was brought up in custody charged with being drunk in charge of a horse and trap on the previous day. Defendant, in reply to the charge said, 'Well, I was the worse for drink, sir'.
>
> Sergt. Bullock said that at about five minutes to six on Tuesday evening he was in Flannel-street, in company with PC Hughes, and saw prisoner driving up Cross-street into High-street; he was swaying about on the seat of the trap, and driving with loose reins. Witness followed prisoner up, and saw him enter the stable yard of the Golden Lion. It was suggested to the prisoner that he should allow his wife to drive, in his place, as he was not fit for it. He made use of very bad language and swore he would knock his wife down if she attempted such a thing. He climbed up into the trap, and fell over the back, and was caught by somebody. Again persuasion was tried, but he was obstinate and drove out of the yard. Witness ordered PC Hughes to stop the horse, and as he tried to do so prisoner struck at him and tried to drive off, flogging the horse with the reins. Finding persuasion no use, prisoner was hauled off to the Police Station. Several farmers attended with the intention of bail, but on seeing him, declined to have anything more to do with it.
>
> Superintendent Davies said that in 20 years he had not had such a noisy troublesome prisoner; he had kept on all night, and had to be deprived of his boots. He didn't want to have him again.
>
> Fined 20s and 4s costs, or 14 days.
>
> The Mayor advised him to sign the pledge.

In 1980, the name was changed to the Sugarloaf, and in 1986 the pub finally closed after 395 years in business.

Publicans: William Lloyd (1591-early seventeenth century), Charles Price (pre-1663), Jenkin Jones (1663), Edward and Elizabeth Rumsey (1667), James James the elder and William Allen (1676), John Greeneheugh (1689), Mr Jones (1787), Jenkin Jones (1791), Thomas Morgan (1803-1804), David Gilbert (1811), E. Taylor (1822), Mary Jayne (1830-1835), William Crump (1839-1844), John Tucker (1850-1853), Mrs Amelia Dew (1858-1865), Mrs Watkins (1868), Edward Lewis (1871-1877), Samuel Peers (1881-1884), Charles Knight (April 1883-1897), James Bell (1901), James Harding (1906), Edmund Evans (1910-1912), Walter Hall (1914-1920), Amos L. Jones (1923-1939), Wilfred and Lena May Walbeoff (1944-1963).

Owners (when known): William Lloyd (1591-early seventeenth century), Thomas William Watkin (1662), John ap William Parry (1662-1663), James James the elder (1663-1676), Jenkin Jones (1791), William Jones (1804), Thomas Jones (1828), 'Jones' (1839), Thomas Jones (1850), 'late Thomas Jones' (1853), Mrs Elizabeth Latham (1859-1873, dead by April 1878), Charles William Latham (1880), Hall's Brewery Co. Ltd (1914), Amos L. Jones (1938).

THE KING WILLIAM, NO. 7, FROGMORE STREET

Listed as a beerhouse in 1862 and as an eating-house in 1865, this pub is first recorded by the name King William in 1868. However, an 1860 listing of a beerhouse owned by the 'late James Powell' may refer to the same place.

In May 1872, Ann Jones – the then licensee – appeared as a witness in a case of theft which resulted from one of her customers, by the name of Curtis, asking another for the loan of a shilling and being given a sovereign by mistake. The case was dismissed. At that time, the pub was still known as the King William. It had certainly closed by December 1873.

Publicans: Enos Lovell (1862), George Harrhy (1864-1868), Ann Jones (May 1872), Benjamin Jones (July 1872).

Owners (when known): 'late James Powell' (1860), 'Parry and others' (1864-1868), John Parry (1872).

THE WHITE HORSE INN, NO. 14, FROGMORE STREET

The sign of the White Horse usually refers to the galloping white horse that was the badge of the royal house of Hanover and dates from after 1714 when George I (the first of that line) came to the throne.

The earliest known publican is the Widow Powell in 1787. Documents of 1785 record the will of Walter Powell, innholder of Abergavenny, and it is possible that 'the Widow Powell' was his wife. In 1825, the pub was the starting point for a Feat of Pedestrianism, which involved walking 66 miles a day for six whole days.

Writing around 1880, 'an Abergavenny Octogenarian' recalled one of the old-time characters associated with the pub:

> I remember a rather singular incident in connection with the interment of the body of a man who
> went by the name of 'Jack o' Breed', in St Mary's Church yard. The man had been an ostler for many
> years at the White Horse, and was a bit of a character in his way. The body had not been buried long
> – not more than a day or two – when it was noticed that the grave had been disturbed, and further
> investigation showed that the grave only contained the shroud and coffin without the lid. A hue and
> cry was raised, and it was ascertained that some young men in the town, several of whom belonged
> to the medical profession, and a few choice and daring spirits had abstracted the body and taken to

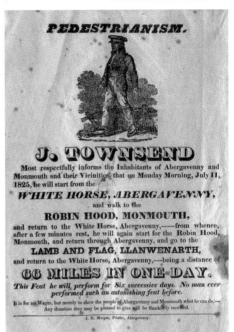

Above left: *The White Horse sometime between 1901 and 1906.*

Above right: *A Feat of Pedestrianism draws custom to the White Horse in 1825.*

the residence of one of the party, for, I suppose, the purpose of dissection. It was said that poor old Jack had himself sold his body to the doctors over and over again for a trifling consideration, and that removal of the body from the grave was merely the fulfilment of which was thought to be a fair and just bargain. However, the resurrectionists were brought to see the grievous mistake they had made, the body was replaced in the coffin.

Always prone to flooding from the Cybi Brook, the pub was finally demolished in 1965.

Publicans: Walter Powell (pre-1785), Widow Powell (1787), John Watkins (1791), William Watkins (1822-1850), Sarah Watkins (1852), David William Watkins (1853-1868), John Harrhy (1871-1895, listed as Hantry in 1875), Jenkin Williams (1901-1906), Stephen Edward Salisbury Baker (1910-1923), William Mort (1926), Benjamin Evans (1934-1965, listed under Blodwen M. Evans in 1938-1939). *Owners* (when known): Walter Powell (pre-1785), William Watkins (1822-1850), David William Watkins (1853-July 1872), Mrs Cadogan (1873), John Harrhy (1880), Rhymney Brewery Co. (1914-1938).

THE OLD HEREFORDSHIRE HOUSE, NO. 25, FROGMORE STREET
(formerly the Crown and Sceptre and the Rose and Crown)
The earliest record of the Rose and Crown dates to 1741, when the publican was Peter Powell, who is described as the 'late Peter Powell' in a mortgage dated 23 May 1769. By that time, the pub was known as the Crown and Sceptre. It is first referred to as the Herefordshire House in 1822, though the name

reverted briefly to the Crown and Sceptre between 1834 and 1839. The pub is first called the Old Herefordshire House in 1842. Confusingly, it is again listed as the Crown and Sceptre in 1850.

A document dated 6 July 1874, which records the sale of a parcel of ground 'at the back of the messuage called the Herefordshire House' names David Roger Jones and Emma Jones, his wife, as the keeping the pub. Although the trade directories list David Roger Jones as the publican of the Herefordshire House between 1873 and 1884, the place actually belonged to his wife, Emma. Her will, dated 5 July 1875, leaves the pub to her daughter, Martha Ann Pritchard, on condition that she allows Mr Jones use of the pub until she 'shall attain the age of twenty one years or the said David Roger Jones shall die whichever shall first happen'.

Emma Jones did not actually die until 15 November 1880. Martha seems to have been her daughter by a previous marriage, possibly to the Thomas Pritchard listed as owning the pub between 1858 and 1868 and described in 1865 as brewer and maltster. By December 1885, David Roger Jones had moved to Newcastle Emlyn in Carmarthenshire.

A photograph in the museum collections, which dates from around 1902-1905 shows the name C.A.W. Prosser painted on the pub as proprietor – this is the only known record of this particular landlord.

A painting of Frogmore Street from around 1850, which was published in the *Abergavenny Chronicle* of 7 October 1949, shows a small cottage standing next to the pub, on the site now occupied by the arch which once led to the back of the premises. Prior to a major rebuild in 1960, it was possible to walk under the arch to stables and a court containing cottages at the rear.

In 1997, the name was changed to the Colonial Inn. It is currently known as the Auberge.

The Old Herefordshire House following a refurbishment in the 1950s.

Publicans: Peter Powell (1747-1769), Mr Edwards (1787), Edward Richards (1791), Richard Cross (1822-1830), Joseph Hobson (1835), Mrs Jones (1839), John Jenks (1842-1853), Thomas Pritchard (1858-1871), David Roger Jones (1873-1884), William John Day (1891), John Maddocks (1895), Mrs Elizabeth Maddocks (1901), C.A.W. Prosser (*c.*1902-1905), George Evans (1906-1914), Christopher Jones (1923), Llewellyn Ashcroft (1926-1939), Mr and Mrs K. Harding (1973).

Owners (when known): David Lewis (1839-1853), 'late David Lewis' (1859-1860), John Grout (1864-1868), Emma Jones (1874-1880), Martha Ann Pritchard (1880-1884), David Roger Jones (May 1914), W.E. Jones (June 1914), Ind Coope & Co. Ltd (1938).

THE BOOT

(now No. 27, Frogmore Street)

This pub stood on the site later covered by the old *Abergavenny Chronicle* offices, where Tesco supermarket now stands. It is only recorded once, in a deed dated 12 December 1741, with William Humphries as publican.

Publicans: William Humphries (1741).

THE BUTCHER'S ARMS, NO. 42, FROGMORE STREET

An early seventeenth-century building, the Butcher's Arms, was demolished in the 1960s. The earliest recorded publican was Joseph Price in 1791. In 1843, the pub was the venue for a meeting of the Abergavenny Society for the Prosecution of Felons. Among the deeds of Nos 17-18 Frogmore Street in the possession of F.L. Nuttall & Co. is a conveyance dated 1 November 1849 and witnessed by Michael Lewis 'of the Butcher's Arms'. In 1852, the publican, Ann Jones, is described as a victualler, flour dealer and corn factor. The landlord in 1858 was one William Williams. He does not seem to have prospered because the Street and Water Rate Book of 1860 contains the note: 'Irrecoverable left the neighbourhood too poor to pay'.

Frogmore Street, c. 1910. The Butcher's Arms is the low, white building on the left with the dormer windows.

George Phillips seems to have done much better. In 1868, he is recorded as the tenant of C.W. Price, but by 1873 he had bought the pub outright. In January 1872, he acted as executor to the will of John Symes of the Railway Hotel on the Brecon Road. Symes had married one of George Phillips' nieces and it is obvious from the family papers in the museum that there was a great deal of tension between her and John Symes' children by a previous marriage (*see* the Railway Hotel).

A bill dated 1885 from George Phillips to a certain 'Mr Gould Esquire' records that it cost 7s 6d to hire a room for a sale and the same amount for the port and sherry consumed there. George Phillips died in December 1908 at the grand old age of eighty-seven and is buried in Llantilio Pertholey churchyard.

By 1938, the pub had been bought by Charles Edwards' brewery of Llanfoist.

Publicans: Joseph Price (1791), Mary Lewis (1822-1823), John Tucker (1830-1844), Michael Lewis (November 1849), John Jones (1850-1851), Ann Jones (1852-1853), William Williams (1858-1859), Thomas Powell (1862), William Thomas (1864), George Phillips (1865-1901), James Jones (1906-1914), John Basham (1920), Arthur Jenkins (1926), A. C. Davies (1934), Mrs Agnes Powell (1937), Margaret Blunt (1938), A.C. Davies (1938-1939), John Tucker (1939), Mrs D. Blunt (1947).
Owners (when known): Joseph Price (1791), William Price (1839), Mary Price (1850-1853), Revd W. Morgan (1859), C.W. Price (1860), W. Morgan (1864), C.W. Price (1868-1872), George Phillips (1873-1914), Charles Edwards Ltd (1938).

THE GEORGE INN, NO. 43, FROGMORE STREET
(formerly the New George and the Little George Tavern)
Referred to in 1787 as the New George (perhaps the Old George in Cross Street had already changed its name by then), the pub was known as the Little George Tavern until 1839. At Christmas 1825, the pub was put up for let and the poster advertising the fact is preserved in the museum:

The George Commercial Hotel sometime between 1876 and 1879. Next door, to the right, is the Butcher's Arms.

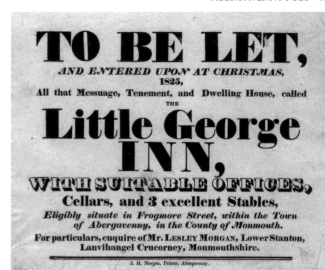

TO BE LET,
AND ENTERED UPON AT CHRISTMAS,
1825,
All that Messuage, Tenement, and Dwelling House, called
THE
Little George
INN,
WITH SUITABLE OFFICES,
Cellars, and 3 excellent Stables,
Eligibly situate in Frogmore Street, within the Town
of Abergavenny, in the County of Monmouth.
For particulars, enquire of Mr. LESLEY MORGAN, Lower Stanton,
Lanvihangel Crucorney, Monmouthshire.

J. H. Morgan, Printer, Abergavenny.

The Little George Inn for let in 1825.

To Be Let, and entered upon at Christmas, 1825, All that Messuage, Tenement and Dwelling House, called The Little George Inn, with suitable offices, Cellars, and 3 excellent Stables, eligibly situate in Frogmore Street.

John Holehouse, the publican in 1830-1839, also ran a stable and a ball court at the rear of the premises. Together with the Angel and the Greyhound, the George was one of Abergavenny's three coaching inns. In 1835, *Pigot's Directory for Monmouthshire* lists the following coach services available from the George:

To Brecon ... the *Fusileer* (from Bristol) calls at the George, every Tuesday, Thursday and Saturday afternoon, at half-past three ... through Crickhowell.
To Bristol, the *Fusileer* (from Brecon) calls at the George, every Monday, Wednesday and Friday morning, at half-past nine; goes through Ragland & Chepstow.
To Hereford, the *Telegraph* ... every Tuesday, Thursday and Saturday at twelve...
To Merthyr Tydvil, the *Royal Mail* ... every afternoon at half-past two.

By 1842, a new coach, *The Prince of Wales*, took passengers to connect with the new London train at Bristol. On 18 October 1837, the Abergavenny Cymreigyddion Society organised an 'ordinary' (a public meal at a fixed time and price) here at four o'clock for visitors to their fourth eisteddfod. The next day, it was held at the Sun Inn in Cross Street. In the 1840s, the ball court was also used as a theatre by travelling companies of actors; in 1841, a play entitled *The Lady of Lyons* was performed.

In the Rate Book dated 30 May 1850, the occupier is Mrs Holehouse and the place is referred to as the Late George Inn. In the 1850s, the pub became known as the George Commercial and Agricultural Hotel and doubled as a posting house. The hotel is listed in the 1873 Rate Book as being owned by J.G. Price but it does not seem to have been occupied. The last known landlord is recorded in 1876 on a petition to the Abergavenny Improvement Commissioners – unfortunately, his signature is illegible.

Publicans: Mr Morgan (1787), J. Phillips (1791), Evan Saunders (1822), John Holehouse (1830-1839), Henry Sanderson (1842-1850), Mrs Holehouse (May 1850), John Ellis (1851-1853), Thomas Price

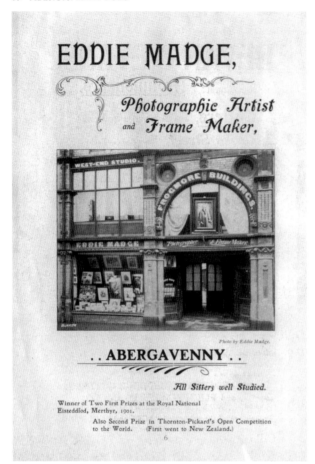

Frogmore Buildings in 1903, the studio of local photographer Eddie Madge.

(1858-1859), Joseph James Stephens (1860-1862), William George Martin (1865), ? Cooke (1872), Robert Acethecca(?) (1876).
Owners (when known): J. Phillips (1791), John Holehouse (1839), Elizabeth Holehouse (1850-1864), J. G. Price (1872-1873).

THE THREE SALMONS, NO. 46, FROGMORE STREET
(also known as the Forester's Welcome)
This pub is referred to as the Three Salmons in 1850, 1851 and 1853. Confusingly, in 1852, there was another Three Salmons in High Street (later called the Guildhall Inn). The Frogmore Street hostelry stood next door but one to the Fountain Inn and, apart from one reference to the place as an eating-house in 1862, it is usually listed simply as a beerhouse. The pub is last recorded in July 1872, when it was known as the Forester's Welcome.

Publicans: William L. Bathurst (1850), William Powell (1851-1853), John Redman (1864) David Williams (1865), Nathaniel Cook (1868), William Jones Jnr (1872).
Owners (when known): William Powell (1850-1864), Nathaniel Cook (1868-1872).

Frogmore Street sometime between 1902 and 1905. The Herefordshire House can be seen on the right, with farmers'
traps parked outside. The Fountain Inn and the Three Salmons are the small, low buildings on the left.

THE GEORGE HOTEL, NO. 47, FROGMORE STREET

(formerly the Fountain Inn)

This pub now forms part of the Richards of Abergavenny hardware store. The earliest recorded publican of the Fountain Inn is William Edwards in 1822. In 1888, the pub, then called the Old Fountain Inn, was put up for sale with the Royal Victoria Brewery (*see* Baker Street). It is described in the sale notice as:

> in the occupation of Mr John Parry as yearly tenant, and comprising: Parlour, kitchen, Tap Room with
> bar, Bagatelle room, three bedrooms and cellar, together with yard, shed and stabling at the rear.

The pub is still referred to in a document of 1898 as the Old Fountain Inn, presumably to differentiate it from the New Fountain in Monk Street. In 1905, the old pub was demolished, rebuilt and renamed the George Hotel.

Publicans: William Edwards (1822), Ann Edwards (1830), John Williams (1835), William Pembridge (1839), Thomas Watkins (1842), David Williams (1850-1865), James Williams (1868-1871), John Parry (1872-1888), Charles Parry (1891-1901), William Denner (1906), Mrs Rosa Denner (1910-1920), James Morris (1914), Benjamin Rees (1920), James McGeever (1923-1926).

Owners (when known): ? Williams (1839), Mary Williams (1850-1853), Elizabeth Williams (1859-1860), E. Williams (1864), Nathaniel Cook (1868-1873), James Gough (1884-1888), Edwin A. Johnson (1914).

The George Hotel, c. 1914.

THE BELL, NO. 50, FROGMORE STREET

Among the deeds to this property in the possession of Mr F.O. Richards is a document dated 16 May 1788, transferring from 'John Watkins of the Parish of Llantilio Pertholey ... Farmer and John Powell of the town of Abergavenny ... Gentleman' to 'John Harris of the same place Mercer':

> the Bell wherein James Powell did heretofore Inhabit and wherein Ann Powell Widow did afterwards dwell and late in the occupation of John Mac'cone.

The same John Powell had sold the Dragon's Head in Nevill Street to John Watkins the previous year (*see* the Dragon's Head).

Publicans: James Powell (pre-1788), Ann Powell (pre-1788), John Mac'cone (1788).
Owners (when known): John Watkins and John Powell (1788), John Harris (1788).

Frogmore Street in the 1920s. On the left, a car is parked outside the Britannia and behind it, on the corner of Baker Street, stands the former Bell Inn.

THE BRITANNIA, NO. 51, FROGMORE STREET

(formerly the Three Kings, the Cock and Horse and the Welsh Guardsman)

Originally known as the Cock and Horse, the earliest record of the pub dates to December 1741, when Benjamin Jenkins left it in trust for his wife Mary and their children. In April 1775, it was sold to Revd Henry Rogers and Walter Williams for the sum of 10s in lieu of repayment of a debt and is described as 'then or late in the tenure ... of one Richard Prichard'.

Henry Rogers and Walter Williams immediately sold the premises for £158 to William Addams, yeoman, his wife, Mary, and Thomas Phillips of Cwmdu. In December 1793, the pub is referred to as the Three Kings, 'otherwise the Cock and Horse'. The pub is first called the Britannia in July 1821, when William Addams sold it to William Fleetwood Bury. The landlord at that time was William Pembridge, who paid an annual rent of £21.

Between 1822 and 1830, the trade directories list William Pembridge as the publican, but as he appears in the St Mary's parish registers as a victualler in Frogmore Street between 4 March 1820 and 31 March 1830, he had probably started in the trade by 1820. By 1839, he had moved to the Fountain Inn, a few doors down.

In March 1823, William Bury left the house in his will to Henry Dyson Gabell of Berkshire, John Fuller of Wiltshire and John Jones of Llansantffraed and, in February 1825, they assigned it to William Addams Williams of Llangibby Castle. By 1833, it was owned jointly by William Addams Williams, Francis MacDonnell of Usk and Caroline Addams Williams, also of Llangibby, who leased the place to David Lewis. A document dated 11 June 1838 describes the pub as 'late in tenure of William Pembridge' at a yearly rent of £24 and 'since in occupation of James Morgan'.

By 1839, David Lewis had become the joint owner with Joseph Roberts of Clodock. At the end of that year they sold it on to Revd William Powell, vicar of Abergavenny. In February 1852, it was sold again, this time to James Parry, farmer, of Great Hardwick and John Cecil, farmer, of Llanrothel, Herefordshire. In October 1868, it was sold to Nathaniel Cook and by 1879 was the property of David Watkins of Lodge Farm, Llwyndu. By the terms of his will, the pub was sold again for the benefit of his wife and sons David, Francis and Joseph and 'other of his children'.

In July 1872, the pub was put up for sale by auction at the Angel Hotel. The advertisement placed in the *Abergavenny Chronicle* for 13 July describes the pub as comprising 'Bar, Two Parlours, Six Bedrooms, Tap Room, Kitchen, Pantry, Brewhouse, Stable, and large Yard'.

By 1928, when it was again put up for sale by auction, the pub was owned by Charles Edwards' Llanfoist Brewery. It is described in the sale particulars as containing a 'Large Tap Room, Smoke Room, Kitchen and lean-to Scullery' on the ground floor with a 'Club Room' upstairs and a '7-tie manger' in the stables at the back. It also had a 'Glazed partition and doors forming Jug and Bottle Department'.

Many local residents have vivid memories of Mr George Steward, one of the former publicans. A veteran of the Boer War under Lord Methuen, Mr Steward was a retired Regimental Sergeant Major and formidable disciplinarian. He was the licensee of the pub from 1914 until 1937, though from October 1934 on it was owned by Godfrey Price and Walter McClure Flinn.

Between 1983 and 1997, the pub was known as the Welsh Guardsman, but reverted to the Britannia in 1997.

Publicans: Richard Prichard (1775), Mr Watkins (1787), Thomas Watkins (1791), William Pembridge (1820-1830), David Lewis (1833), Thomas Whiting (1835), James Morgan (pre-1838), John Ball (1839), William Williams (1842-1844), Walter James (1850), Thomas S. Rowes (1853), John Havard (1858-1860), Thomas Evans Parry (1862), William Prosser (1865-1880), Miss Mary Ann Prosser (1884), Benjamin Jones (1891), Mrs Annie Jones (1895), Charles William Prosser (1901-1906), Soloman Francis (1910-May 1914), George B. Steward (1914-1939), Bill King (1983-1994).

Owners (when known): Benjamin Jenkins (1741), Revd Henry Rogers and Walter Williams (1775), William and Mary Addams and Thomas Phillips (1775-1821), William Fleetwood Bury (1821-1823), Henry Dyson Gabell, John Fuller and John Jones (1823-1825), William Addams Williams, Francis MacDonnell and Caroline Addams Williams (1825-1833), David Lewis (1833-1839) and Joseph Roberts (1839), Revd William Powell (1839-1852), John Cecil (1852) and James Parry (1852-1868), Nathaniel Cook (1868), David Watkins (1879), Joseph Watkins (1914), William Lewis, James Price and David Powell (1934), Godfrey Price and Walter McClure Flinn (1934), Charles B. Steward (1938).

THE GRIFFIN INN, NO. 59, FROGMORE STREET
(formerly the British Lion)
The name of this house changed from the British Lion to the Griffin Inn sometime between 1853 and 1858. The pub is marked on Wood's 1834 map of Abergavenny, though the earliest known publican is Edward Taylor in 1835. The pub seems to have declined as the nineteenth century wore on – its rateable value dropped from £23 in 1839 to just £14 10s. in 1873. The Griffin, together with the Star in Crickhowell, is among the property listed in the will of Elizabeth Window, widow, dated 27 March 1875.

By 1938, the pub had been taken over by the Cheltenham Original Brewery. The business ceased trading as a public house in the early 1950s.

Publicans: Edward Taylor (1835), Thomas Evans (1839), John Hevens (1842-1850), John Watkins Taylor (1850-1852), William Phillips (1853-1860), Mrs Susan Phillips (1862-1872, listed as Sarah in 1864),

The Griffin Inn in 1907.

John Garstone (1873-1875), Mrs Susan Garstone (1884), John Rosser (1891-1926), Thomas Edwards (1934-1947, listed under S. Edwards in 1939).
Owners (when known): Thomas Evans (1839), Thomas Baker (1850-June 1851), James Gilbert (July 1851-1853), George Window (1859-1872), Mrs Elizabeth Window (1873-1875), John Rosser (1914), Cheltenham Original Brewery (1938).

THE WELCOME TEMPERANCE HOTEL, NO. 60, FROGMORE STREET
(formerly the Imperial Temperance Hotel and the Abergavenny Temperance Hotel)
The earliest record of the Abergavenny Temperance Hotel dates to 1875, with M. Havard as proprietor. By 1884, the place had been taken over by Evan Jones and re-named the Imperial Temperance Hotel. Evan Jones also provided refreshments in the castle grounds. The *Burrow's 1903 Official Handbook to Abergavenny* includes an advertisement describing the place as the Imperial Commercial Temperance Hotel and Coffee Tavern. The advert also mentions that: 'Omnibuses pass the door regularly. Accommodation with comfort and attention at Moderate Charges. Lock-up Cycle House.'

The lock-up cycle house was behind Davies' butchers shop, which stood on the other side of the road at No. 9a Frogmore Street. By 1912, the hotel was in the hands of Frank Morris. Between 1923 and 1933, the business is recorded as the Welcome Temperance Hotel and Café, with T. Webb ('Baker and Confectioner – Bride and Christening Cakes made to order') as proprietor.

Proprietors: M. Havard (1875-1877), Evan Jones (1884-1910), Frank J. D. Morris (1912-1921), T. Webb (1923-1933).

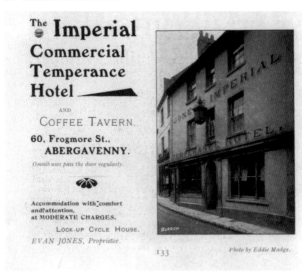

The Imperial Temperance Hotel in 1903

THE KING DAVID INN, NO. 62, FROGMORE STREET

The pub is first recorded in 1791, with Ann Jones as publican. It next appears in a deed of 1800, when it was bought by Thomas Jones, gentleman of Abergavenny, from Sir George Chad and John Hanbury Williams. By 1828, Thomas Jones also owned the Golden Lion. By 1879, the inn could provide stabling for twenty horses and was being let at £4 per annum.

In August 1897, the pub was offered for sale by auction and is described in the sale particulars as:

> on the Ground Floor, Bar, Smoke Room, Tap Room, Kitchen, Scullery and Larder; on the First Floor, Sitting Room and One Bedroom, and on the Second Floor, Landing and Two Bedrooms. At the rear are Yard and Brew-house ... with Stabling for about Twenty Horses... It has and always will command a good trade, and ... is Celebrated for its Home Brewed Ale.

The pub is also described as one of the 'best frequented houses in the town'. It had been held by Edward Games Morgan under a 21-year repairing lease since 25 March 1883, even though the 1884 trade directory lists the landlord as Charles Knight. It is likely that the directories were prepared some time in advance and that by the time it came out, Mr Knight had left!

From 1926 onwards, the pub was kept by Mr Edward 'Ted' Bowen, who brewed his own beer and cider on the premises. His cider was sent as far as Blackpool at 1s 6d per gallon! On the premises it cost 6d a pint, while home-brewed beer could be enjoyed for a mere 3d. In 1944, the pub was sold to Roberts Breweries of Aberystwyth, who in turn sold out to Anglo Breweries in 1947. The pub finally closed in 1973.

Publicans: Ann Jones (1791), D. Mosley (1822), William Powell (1830-1844), Richard James (1850-1853), James Skyrm (1858-1859), ? Symes (1860), Mrs Harriet Lewis (1862-1868), Isaac Griffiths (1871-1877), Charles Knight (1884, listed in the trade directory), Edward Games Morgan (March 1883-1901), Mrs Emily Morgan (1906), John Samuel Jones (1908-1923), Edward J. Bowen (1926-1939).
Owners (when known): Thomas Jones (1800-1839), Thomas Jones (1850-June 1851), 'late T. Jones' (July 1851-1853), Mrs Elizabeth Latham (1859-1873, dead by April 1878), Charles William Latham (1880), John Samuel Jones (1914), Edward J. Bowen (1938), Roberts Ltd Brewers (1944-1947), Anglo Breweries (1947).

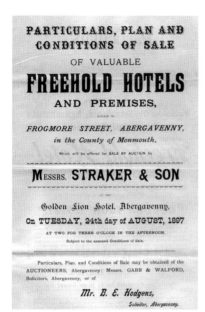

PARTICULARS, PLAN AND
CONDITIONS OF SALE

OF VALUABLE

FREEHOLD HOTELS

AND PREMISES,

FROGMORE STREET, ABERGAVENNY,
in the County of Monmouth,

Which will be offered for SALE BY AUCTION by

MESSRS. STRAKER & SON

Golden Lion Hotel, Abergavenny,

On TUESDAY, 24th day of AUGUST, 1897

AT TWO FOR THREE O'CLOCK IN THE AFTERNOON,
Subject to the annexed Conditions of Sale.

Particulars, Plan and Conditions of Sale may be obtained of the
AUCTIONEERS, Abergavenny; Messrs. GABB & WALFORD,
Solicitors, Abergavenny, or of

Mr. B. E. Hodgens,
Solicitor, Abergavenny.

Left and below: *A plan of the King David and the Golden Lion in 1897.*

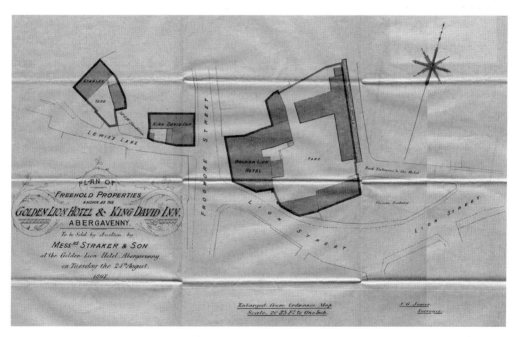

PLAN OF
FREEHOLD PROPERTIES
KNOWN AS THE
GOLDEN LION HOTEL & KING DAVID INN.
ABERGAVENNY.
To be Sold by Auction by
MESS.RS STRAKER & SON
at the Golden Lion Hotel, Abergavenny,
on Tuesday the 24th August.
1897.

Enlarged from Ordnance Map.
Scale, 20·83 Ft. to One Inch.

J. G. James,
Surveyor.

THE LAMB INN, NOS 63-4, FROGMORE STREET

(formerly the Star and Garter)

The earliest record of the Star and Garter dates to 29 February 1747, when James Jones, 'hair bleacher', bequeathed all his real estate to his wife, Ann 'except all that messuage called the Starr and Garter situate in Frogmore Street'. In September 1741, he had taken out a lease from Elizabeth Schnell of London on the 'site of dwelling houses where Joan Price, Eleanor Watkins widow and Morgan Leonard once lived' and this is almost certainly the site later occupied by the pub.

*The King David Inn
(on the right) in 1908.*

A codicil to this will, dated 15 February 1751, states that for payment of £160 to his widow on his death, his son-in-law, John Jones of Abergavenny, maltster, would then own the pub and another tenement then in the possession of John Watkins and David Watkins. James Jones's will was finally proved in April 1751, with the pub was still occupied by John Watkins.

The pub is first called the Lamb Inn in a marriage agreement, dated 22 June 1775, between Matthew Wilson and Elizabeth, daughter of John Watkins 'of the Lamb, inn holder'. In January 1780, John Watkins, still the innholder, acted as agent for Matthew Wilson in leasing out a parcel of land. By 1784, the pub was owned by Margaret, James Jones's daughter, but was still 'in the possession of John Watkins'. He was still publican in 1787, but by 1791, the pub was being run by Thomas Evans.

In August 1803, the Lamb (together with the Golden Lion opposite) was put up for sale by a group of trustees. It is described in the advertisement as having a 'Drinking Room, Cellaring, Malting House'. The sitting tenant was Evan Evans, whose annual rent was £31 10s. In December 1803, an agreement was drawn up to sell the pub to Lutley Barnaby, Esquire, of Llangua for £420 but the sale seems not to have taken place. The Lamb was finally sold to John Lewis, the ironmonger, in June 1804. He converted the pub into the ironmongery and foundry that was to give its name to Lewis' Lane.

In 1831, a dispute arose between John Lewis and Baker Gabb (the Monk Street solicitor) over a right of way over two strips of land 'formerly called the Lamb Yard or Green'. It is obvious that Lamb Yard was the old name for what is now Lewis' Lane.

Publicans: John Watkins (1750-1787), Thomas Evans (1791), Evan Evans (1803-1804).
Owners (when known): James Jones (1747-1751), John Jones (1751), Margaret Jones (1784), Trustees (1803).

Other pubs in Frogmore Street, whose exact whereabouts are not known, include:

THE BLACK SWAN

The Black Swan is recorded as early as 1787. In October 1795, part of the premises was demolished to widen Frogmore Street, and the publican, Mr Jenkin Jones, received a payment of £20 from the Abergavenny Improvement Commissioners in compensation. He was also allowed to appropriate the materials for his own use.

*Frogmore Street
and High Street in
the early twentieth
century. Oliver's
stood on the site of
the old Lamb Inn.*

In 1818, the Commissioners issued a notice to 'Joseph Williams of the Black Swan to stop up the Trap Door in Front of his Dwelling House in Frogmore Street'.

Publicans: Widow Bevan (1787), Elizabeth Bevan (1791), Jenkin Jones (1795), Joseph Williams (1818).
Owners: Jenkin Jones (1795).

THE BEAR INN
Two documents, dated 1 January and 2 January 1744, name William Bradshaw as the owner of the 'Bear Inn, Frogmore Street, now or late in the occupation of Ann Powell, widow'.

Publicans: Ann Powell (1744).
Owners: William Bradshaw (1744).

THE STAR

Publicans: Joseph Jayne (1822–1823), Michael Power (1830)

THE RED CROSS

Publicans: Mr Watkins (1787).

BEERHOUSES
The following beer retailers are recorded in Frogmore Street. Unfortunately we do not know the exact locations of their houses: William Griffiths (1835), Edwin Lewis (1835), Thomas Farrell (1850, also acted as a carrier to Hereford, Gloucester and Newport), Eliza Jones (1858).

BREWERS
Richard Stone (1835).

HEREFORD ROAD

THE VICTORIA INN, HEREFORD ROAD
(formerly the Mason's Arms)
First recorded in 1835, with Henry Watkins as publican, the tavern was originally known as the Mason's Arms. The name changed to the Victoria Inn sometime between 1844 and 1850.

The *Abergavenny Chronicle* for 13 July 1872 records that the landlord, William Watkins, was charged with 'selling excisable liquors during prohibited hours' (i.e. on a Sunday):

> The Bench said ... that all the men in the house were drunk, and they were sorry to hear of such conduct, which they were determined to put a stop to, and fined defendant 40s and costs. The money was paid. Defendant said it was a hard case that a master cannot keep his workmen in the house on a Sunday.

Although the inn closed in 1990 due to subsidence, the premises were renovated and reopened in 1992 as the Bailey.

Publicans: Henry Watkins (1835), James Pillinger (1839), John Rosser (1840), Henry Watkins (1842), William Watkins (1850-July 1872), Matthew Tombs (1873-1877), Henry Jeffreys (1884-1914), Charles Walter Logan (1923), Stephen Edward Salisbury Baker (1926-1937), W.H. Waller (1938), J.A. Edwards (1939).
Owners (when known): William Watkins (1839-1868), Matthew Tombs (1873), Henry Jeffreys (1914), W.H. Waller (1938).

BEER RETAILERS (LOCATIONS UNKNOWN)
John Ellis (1842-1844), John Morgan Edmunds (1850; *see* Monk Street).

PORTER DEALERS (LOCATIONS UNKNOWN)
James W. Harvey (1858).

HIGH STREET

THE GREYHOUND HOTEL, NO. 4, HIGH STREET
In its heyday, this rather grand hotel was a substantial building containing eighteen bedrooms, four reception rooms, a bar, a ballroom and a 150-seat dining room. Incredibly, the 'long bar' was fully 25 yards in length.

In 1787, the publican was a Mr C. Wallington. By 1791, Ann Wallington was both publican and freeholder. From 1794 onwards, the Abergavenny Improvement Commissioners often used the place as the venue for their official meetings. In 1800, the Abergavenny Society for the Prosecution of Felons also met at the Greyhound.

Together with the Angel and the George Inn in Frogmore Street, the Greyhound was one of Abergavenny's three coaching inns. In 1835, *Pigot's Directory for Monmouthshire* lists the following coach services available from the Greyhound:

> To London ... the *Paul Pry* (from Carmarthen) ... every morning (Sunday excepted) at half-past twelve; all go through Ragland and Monmouth.
> To Carmarthen, the *Paul Pry* (from London) ... every afternoon (Sunday excepted) at one; goes

through Crickhowell.

To Merthyr Tydvil ... the *Tally-Ho* ... every Tuesday, Thursday & Saturday afternoon at 4.

By 1839, the freehold was held by the Duke of Beaufort. In August 1849, the hotel was put up for sale and is described in the sale particulars as:

> containing numerous rooms and conveniences, with yards, stabling for twenty horses, coach houses and every convenience for carrying on an extensive trade. These premises are on lease granted to Mrs Hickman (but now in the occupation of Mr William Morgan).

On census night 1851, business was obviously slack; those registered as in residence including the proprietor Timothy Bluck, his wife, five children, five servants and only two guests! In 1852, the Greyhound is described as a Family, Commercial, Agricultural Hotel and Posting House!

By 1853, the hotel was being run by Phillip Morgan, who would later also become the proprietor of the Angel Hotel in Cross Street. By 1854, the hotel was offering a horse-omnibus service to connect with the newfangled railways and, from 1862, doubled as the Inland Revenue office (William Herring was the inspector in 1871).

The Tucker family seems to have acquired the Greyhound sometime between 1865 and 1868 and various members of the family were to run the business from then until at least 1882. By July 1872, William Tucker had extended the hotel and added the new Tap and Billiard Room in Market Street, which is now known as the Greyhound Vaults. In the area behind the Vaults, the hotel even had its own bowling green.

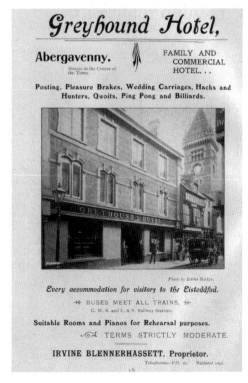

The Greyhound in 1903.

A brochure dating from the 1940s gives detailed descriptions of the facilities the Greyhound was able to offer:

> Accommodation comprises a spacious Coffee Room, a Sitting room (resident guests only), a Smoke room, Commercial Room, and eighteen Bedrooms all with hot and cold water fittings. The Bar is a cosy rendezvous. Special arrangements for wedding parties and other special functions are made in the large private Dining Room.

Local resident Peter Coleman had fond memories of the old place:

> down through the centre of the hotel was a passageway which ran from the back right through to the High Street, and leading off this passageway were the bars and the various rooms of the hotel, an hotel which was heavy in polished mahogany and brass, with great long bars, dining rooms, smoke rooms, lounges and, right at the rear, a dance hall. I don't know how many dances and parties we attended at that place. It was the home of one of the old time dancing groups in Abergavenny and how we used to love to go there to dance to Joe Davies's orchestra. We thoroughly enjoyed ourselves.

By 1901, the hotel was owned by R.P. Culley and Co. Ltd, a firm of wine merchants and 'refreshment contractors' based in Cardiff. The hotel finally closed in 1959.

Publicans: Mr C. Wallington (1787), Mrs Ann Wallington (1791-1794), John Strange (1811), Thomas Evans (1822-1823), George Evans (1830-1835), ? Hickman (1839), John Richards (1842-1844), William Morgan (1849), Timothy Bluck (1850-1852), Phillip Morgan (1853-1865), Mrs Tucker (1868), William Tucker (1871-1880), Mrs Emily Tucker (1882, dead by 1884), Walter C. Williams (1891-1895), Francis Albert McGraith (1901), R.P. Culley & Co. (1901-1906; Francis A. McCraith was manager in 1906), Mrs Emily M. Tovell (1910-1914), Mrs Ethel Maude Reynolds (1920), Rees, Rogers and Co. (1923-1926), C.C. Daft (1927-1931), Mrs M. Cotton (manageress, 1934).

Owners (when known): Ann Wallington (1791), Duke of Beaufort (1839), Mrs Hickman (1849), Duke of Beaufort (1850-1851), Robert Williams (1853-1864), S.W. Tucker (1868), William Tucker (1872), S.W. Tucker (1873), William Tucker (1880), R.P. Culley and Co. (1901-1914), Rees, Rogers and Co. (1923-1926), Greyhound Co. Ltd (1938).

THE VICTORIA TEMPERANCE HOTEL, NO. 6, HIGH STREET

Originally a saddler's shop and, later, a jeweller's business, the earliest record of the Victoria Temperance Hotel dates to 1901, with Charles H. Sayce as proprietor. He also ran a restaurant at No. 21, Frogmore Street. From 1937 until 1961, Alec Sayce ran the business as the Victoria Café and Hotel. The Sayces were still the freeholders in 1984.

Proprietors: Charles H. Sayce (1901-1914), Fred Woodhead (1923-1931).

THE GUILDHALL INN, NO. 14, HIGH STREET

(formerly the Three Salmons)

In the 1851 census returns, Elisha Watkins is recorded as a brewer and maltster occupying these premises and he also appears in the 1852 trade directory as 'maltster, brewer, and beer retailer, Three Salmons, High Street'. This is the only time the pub is listed by that name. He had also been running

These photographs of the Greyhound are taken from a brochure published in the 1940s. This picture shows the entrance hall.

The lounge bar of the Greyhound.

The Greyhound's dining room

the brewery in Lion Street formerly occupied by William Ellis (*see* Ellis' Brewery) since at least 1850. An Elisha Watkins is recorded as a brewer as early as 1818, when his wife, Sarah, died. Unfortunately, we do not know whether this is the same man or where his premises were at that time.

By 1860, with John Gethin James as publican, the pub was called simply the Guildhall. He also worked as a land agent and surveyor. By 1865, the premises were known as the Guildhall Wine and Spirits Vault. By 1868, the pub (now known as the Guildhall Hotel) was under the management of John Harrhy who, according to a bill preserved in the museum, charged a certain Lloyd Powell, Esquire some £2 14s 6d for a cask of brandy and 4s 6d for a bottle of the same poison.

A document dated 28 November 1882 records that John Lewis, who lived at No. 21, Victoria Street, was the owner of 'a certain house and premises ... generally known by the name of The Guildhall Inn' and had leased the pub to James Gimlett for five years. John Lewis agreed that on expiry of the lease he would allow the Abergavenny Improvement Commissioners (who were 'desirous of effecting certain improvements by widening a portion of the said street') 'to take down the front of the said House and premises and to rebuild the same upon a new front line'. The work commenced in 1887 and the building has changed very little since.

By the 1920s, the pub was once again known as the Guildhall Vaults. The last known publican was William Eustence and the premises closed in 1921. In the days before the advent of electric street lighting, the Guildhall was very poorly lit and at least one of Abergavenny's senior citizens has a very vivid, if painful, memory of falling over the front step late at night!

Publicans: Elisha Watkins (1851-1852), John Gethin James (1860-1865), John Harrhy and Mrs Harrhy (1868), James W. Tranter (1872-1875), John Stepney (1876), J.C. Harrhy (1879), William James Gimlett (1880-1882), Philip Price (1884-1895), Henry Lewis (1901), Thomas George Jones (1906), William Scott (1910), William John Eustence (1914), Charles Davies (1920), William John Eustence (1921).
Owners (when known): William Jones (1851-1860), Mrs Jones (1868-1872), John Lewis (1873-1882), Henry Jeffreys (1914).

LION STREET

THE NEW MARKET INN, NO. 22, LION STREET
The New Market Inn formerly stood on the site of the Lion Street entrance to the lower market car park (still called New Market Close). On the 1834 map of Abergavenny, the site is shown as a steam mill. Between 1850 and 1853, the place was a brewery run by Samuel Trotter, leased from Henry C. Williams. Between 1859 and 1864, it is recorded as a brewery and malthouse owned by E. G. Lewis.

The earliest recorded publican is William Poole in 1865. In July 1872, the place is listed as a pub and brewery run by Frederick Coombs and owned by the Misses Lewis. Later, the pub was bought by Facey's Brewery, who used the old brewery as a malthouse.

Publicans: William Poole (1865), Elizabeth Trew (1868), John Davies (1871), Frederick Coombs (1872-1877), Thomas Bryan (1884-1901), Thomas James Lloyd (1906-1914), Miss Lily Bath (1923), Edgar Thomas (1926), Mrs Ella Rosina Watkins (1934), William Morgan Thomas (1937-1939).
Owners (when known): E.G. Lewis (1859-1868), Misses Lewis (1872), E.G. Lewis (1873), S.H. Facey & Son Ltd (1914-1939)

THE ROYAL OAK, NOS 30-32, LION STREET

The earliest reference to a pub called the Royal Oak in Abergavenny is found in a document dated 22 March 1749, when it was owned by John Hanbury of London. Unfortunately, we do not know where this house stood. In 1787, a pub of the same name is listed in Monk Street with a Mr Trew as publican. Valentine Trew is listed in 1791. If this is the same as the Royal Oak in Lion Street (which seems likely), then it was built sometime between 1775 and 1787 by a Thomas Watkins on a piece of garden land formerly in the occupation of William Evans, shoemaker, and his wife Gwenllian.

In February 1809, the pub was leased to Phillip Phillips, who sold it on in June 1810 to Barnett Chance Oakley 'late of Crickhowell co. Brecon, but now of Abergavenny, inn holder, and Elizabeth his wife'. In November 1810, the pub was bought by Sir John Edward Harrington of London for £228. Finally, on St David's Day 1821, the place was bought by William Watkins of Abergavenny, gentleman. By that time, it had ceased trading as a public house.

Publicans: Mr Trew (1787), Valentine Trew (1791), Phillip Phillips (1809-1810), Barnett Chance Oakley (1810).
Owners (when known): Thomas Watkins (1775), Phillip Phillips (1809-1810), Sir John Edward Harrington (1809-1821), William Watkins (1821-1859).

The former New Market Inn in 1967. By this time, it was owned by Eagle Star Insurance.

Nos 30-32, Lion Street in 1967. From 1787 to 1810, this was the Royal Oak.

THE FARMER'S ARMS, NO. 34, LION STREET

The smaller lounge section of the present pub marks the original extent of the licensed premises. The first recorded publican is William Watkins in 1865. On 4 November 1885, James Straker sold the pub by auction at the Greyhound Hotel 'together with an Eligible Building Site thereto adjoining ... now in the occupation of Mr Abraham Caddick as yearly tenant'. The larger part of the pub on the corner of Market Street was almost certainly added shortly after. The plot of land on which it was built was the site of the original Bethany Baptist Chapel until 1883, when it was pulled down and rebuilt in its current position.

In 1996, the name changed to the Market Tafarn.

Publicans: William Watkins (1865-1868), William Spencer (1871), Thomas Denner (1872-1877), Abraham Alexander Caddick (1884-1885), Benjamin Tomkins (1891), Charles Prosser (1895), Giles Hooper (1901), Thomas Brown (1906), Mrs Elizabeth Phillips (1910-1914), Edward James Bowen (1923), John Edwards (1926), Percy H. Harris (1934-1939).
Owners (when known): James Hart (1868-1873, described as 'late' in 1873), Catherine Treharne (1914), Charles Edwards' Brewery Ltd (1938).

The Farmer's Arms sometime between 1910 and 1914.

The Farmer's Arms in 1967. It was then a Rhymney Brewery house.

THE BLACK LION, NO. 36, LION STREET

(formerly the Plough Inn and the Lion Street Tavern)

The Black Lion started as a beerhouse and the earliest record of the place dates to 1851 when the publican was Joseph Rogers. In 1852, it was called the Lion Tavern. By 1858, the pub had become part of William Morgan's brewing empire (*see* the Phoenix Brewery) and was known as the Lion Street Tavern. For a short period between 1862 and 1865, it was known as the Plough Inn. The earliest reference to the place as the Black Lion dates to 1867 when the pub, which had recently been rebuilt 'in a very substantial manner', was put up for sale. At the time, it was occupied by Joseph Stanley, at an annual rent of £50.

Between January 1880 and August 1882, Edwin Sheen, the local builder, did a great deal of work at the Black Lion, all of which is outlined in his bill to Joseph Stanley, which survives in the museum collection. The works carried out included 'Building Shed and pigstyes' in the adjoining field (now covered by the solicitor's offices in Tiverton Place) in January 1880; 'alterations to New Room Stairs and doorway and New doorway into Brewhouse' in November of the same year; 'Taking down Kitchen Ranges and rebuilding same' in November 1881 and, finally, 'Building New Dairy' in April 1882. The total cost amounted to £42 14s 1½d.

Publicans: Joseph Rogers (1851–died 1854), Joseph Stanley (1858–1891), Mrs Margaret Stanley (1895), Mrs Margaret Gameson (1901–1921), Mrs Annie Maud Murphy (1923), Frederick Henry Wood (1926–1937), I.P. Stanley (1938–1939).
Owners (when known): Captain Roberts (1851–1853), William Morgan (1858–1914), I.P. Stanley (1938).

The Black Lion in 1967.

THE GREEN DRAGON, LION STREET

The earliest record of the Green Dragon is in a document dating from 1694, when it was occupied by Elizabeth Grimes. It describes the pub as being:

> situated in Frogmore Street Abergavenny and extending in front from the gate there called Frogmore Street Gate, to the lane there called Kybby Lane, to the town wall and the Kybby Brook

In January 1824, William, Elizabeth and Ebenezer Harris, Revd Micah Thomas and Isaac Wyke leased the pub to James Harris of Bristol for one year. The last known landlord was William Williams in 1862.

Publicans: Elizabeth Grimes (1694), Mrs Price (1787), Roger Powell (1791), D. Williams (1822-1823), Thomas Jones (1830), Joshua Morgan (1835-1839), Elisha Watkins (1842-June 1851), James Williams (July 1851-1860), William Williams (1862).
Owners (when known): William Harris, Elizabeth Harris, Ebenezer Harris, Revd Micah Thomas and Isaac Wyke (1824), Mr Harris (1839), E. Harris (1850-1851), 'late S. Harris' (1853), 'Thomas and others' (1859), 'Conway and others' (1860).

BEERHOUSES

In 1868, two other beerhouses are recorded in Lion Street, though their exact whereabouts are not known. They were both owned by the brewer, William Morgan and were run by W. Rees and James Sayce respectively. One of them may have been the beer shop which stood next to Morgan's Brewery (*see pp80-1*) and which was sold in 1867. In the sale particulars, it is described as being 'occupied by William Ross ... at the yearly rent of £16'. It had a cider warehouse at the back.

S.J. Ruther's in 1935, the site of the old Green Dragon. Ellis' Brewery can be seen in the background.

ELLIS' BREWERY, HORSINGTON'S YARD

In February 1827, an advert appeared for 'a newly fitted up Retail Brewery capable of brewing twenty barrels per week, with an excellent range of cellars, with, or without a good malt house adjoining, so situated in a cool shade as to be worked for ten months in the year'. The owner was Isaac Wyke, a local apothecary and treasurer of the Welsh and English Baptist Education Society that ran the Baptist Academy in Pen y Pound. The new brewery was rented by William Ellis and the lease, dated 26 February 1827, describes it as then being in the occupation of John Pritchard 'with the malt house and brewery adjoining situate in a court ... formerly called Mr Roger's Court'. By 1830, it was known as Hanover Court.

By 1839, William Ellis was building a new brewery on a plot of land near the Grofield Inn in Baker Street. It opened shortly after and was called the Royal Victoria Brewery (*see* Baker Street).

Between 1850 and 1852, the Lion Street brewery was owned and run by Elisha Watkins, who also ran the Three Salmons in High Street. He had started his career as the publican of the nearby Green Dragon, where he is recorded from 1842 until 1850. In 1853, the brewery was owned by James Hardman, though by 1857 part of the site had been taken over by Tucker's Steam Flour Mills. James Hardman also owned a house in High Street next to what was later to become the Guildhall Inn. He was still running the brewery when it was last recorded in 1860.

After this, it is probable that the site was completely taken over by the Tuckers. They in turn gave way in 1907 to the Horsington Brothers, who utilised the site as a builder's stores. The area, though officially in Lion Street, is still known as Horsington's Yard.

Brewers: William Ellis (1827-1839), Elisha Watkins (1850-1852), James Hardman (1853-1860).
Owners (when known): Isaac Wyke (1827), Mrs Wyke (1839), Elisha Watkins (1850), James Hardman (1853-1860).

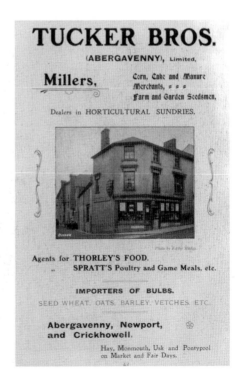

Tucker Bros mill in 1903. In the foreground is the site of the old Green Dragon. The large building on the left is Ellis' Brewery.

Above and left: *Ellis' Brewery in a sorry state, c. 1960. From 1907 to 1960, the building was used as a builders' yard by Horsington Bros, hence the modern name – Horsington's Yard.*

WILLIAM MORGAN AND CO. BREWERY, TIVERTON PLACE

(formerly the Phoenix Brewery, the Old Brewery and the Old Abergavenny Brewery)

The Phoenix Brewery (as it was originally known) stood on the site now covered by the Tiverton Place car park in Lion Street. In around 1880, 'an Abergavenny Octogenarian' recalling his youth wrote:

> After the destruction [by fire] of the warehouse in Tiverton-place a brewery was erected on the site by Messrs. Morgan and Wheeley. That was the first brewery built in Abergavenny.

The fire must have been in 1822, as a document in the museum collections dated 2 January 1823 records the agreement of a 21-year lease between Revd William Roberts 'of Eton College in the

A Phoenix Brewery letterhead from 1832.

County of Buckingham', Charles Wheeley, banker and William Morgan, maltster, 'the said Charles Wheeley and William Morgan intending to erect a brewery and commence the business of Brewers'. They were to pay an annual rent of £15 for 'the buildings lately damaged by fire' and then to spend 'five hundred pounds ... in making such additions and alterations ... as may render them suitable to the purposes of a Brewery'.

Their landlord having learned a painful lesson, they were also required to insure the premises against 'loss by fire ... in the full sum of three hundred pounds'. Their phoenix really would arise from the ashes!

The partnership between Morgan and Wheeley continued until August 1832, when Charles Wheeley died and the brewery was taken over by Morrison and Co. One of their receipts dated to that year survives in the museum. In those days, a firkin of ale cost 9s 9d. Wood's map of 1834 shows the brewery as Morrison and Co. and they are listed in *Pigot's Directory* for 1835.

However, in March 1839, the brewery was once again leased, this time by John Walter Roberts of Surrey, 'a Captn. in Her Majesty's Royal Navy', to William Morgan (who was then living in The Hill). He promptly leased the brewery on to Thomas Gratrex, banker, and William Morgan the Younger, and the new Abergavenny Brewery Co. was established on 18 May 1840, with shares issued for sale at £100 a piece. The brewery is referred to in 1842 and 1844 as the Old Brewery. By 1847, William Morgan the Younger was living at Pen y Causeway (now The Elms in Belmont Road). Sometime between 1853 and 1859, Morgan and Co. seem to have bought the brewery site outright from the Roberts family.

Very early on, William Morgan and Co. set about buying public houses in Abergavenny, presumably to sell the beer produced at the brewery. William Morgan loaned money to the landlord of the Prince Albert (later the Carpenter's Arms) in Baker Street in 1845, perhaps with a view to increasing his own sales. He is also recorded as the owner of no less than seven pubs and beerhouses at various times: the Bull Inn in St John's Square in 1839, the Market House Tavern (later the Market Tavern) in Market Street from 1855 to 1867, the Lion Street Tavern (later the Black Lion) in 1858, the Angler's Arms in

Mill Street in 1860 and the Blorenge Inn (later the Belmont Inn) and two beerhouses in Lion Street in 1868.

By December 1867, the brewery, described as the Old Abergavenny Brewery, was unoccupied and the site was sold 'subject to a right of way or back entrance to the old Bank premises'. In 1873, the Abergavenny Water Rates Book records the water bill for building Tiverton Place on the brewery site, which was then owned by E. Tucker.

Brewers: William Morgan and Charles Wheeley (1823-1832), Morrison and Co. (1832-1835), William Morgan and Co. (1839-1867).
Owners (when known): Revd William Roberts (1823), Captain John Walter Roberts (1839-1853), William Morgan (1859-1867), E. Tucker (1873).

OTHER BREWERIES IN LION STREET
John Brock (later of the Market House Tavern) is recorded in the St Mary's parish registers as a brewer in 'Lion Lane' between October 1832 and February 1840. We do not know the exact whereabouts of his brewery.

MARKET STREET

THE MARKET TAVERN, NO. 11, MARKET STREET
(also known as the Market House Tavern)
The pub is first recorded in 1850 as the Market House Tavern, with John Brock as publican. It was owned by William Morgan of the Phoenix Brewery. John Brock was originally from Devon and is recorded in the St Mary's parish registers as a brewer in Monk Street in July 1830 and in Lion Street between October 1832 and February 1840. He is also listed as a beer retailer in Lion Street between 1842 and 1844. The exact site of his brewery and beerhouse is not known.

In 1859, the pub is referred to as the Market Tavern but seems to have reverted to the original name again by 1860. The pub was sold in 1867, with Henry Ruther as publican. His annual rent stood at £40. In 1868, the name was changed permanently to the Market Tavern and William Marston and his wife Mary Anna Price reconveyed the premises to Messrs Thomas Gratrex and William Morgan the Younger. Trading ceased in 1962.

Publicans: John Brock (1850-1853), William Cooke (1858), William Rowley (1859), Thomas Powell (1860), Edwin Smith (1862), T. Williams (1864), Henry J. Ruther (1867-1884), George Simmons (1891-1895), John George Herbert (1901), John Storey (1906-1923), Mrs Leonora J. Storey (1926), John Storey (1926-1939).
Owners (when known): William Morgan (1850-1867), William Marston and Mary Ann Price (1868), Thomas Gratrex and William Morgan the Younger (1868), ? Underwood (1872), Lewis Williams (1873), Charles Edwards Brewery Ltd (1914-1938).

FACEY'S BREWERY, OLD BREWERY YARD
Samuel Henry Facey, a saddler from Brecon, had set up in business as a wine and spirit merchant in the White Swan in Cross Street by January 1864. After a brief partnership with Frank Morgan at the Brecon Road brewery in 1871 and 1872, he opened his own brewery in Market Street sometime

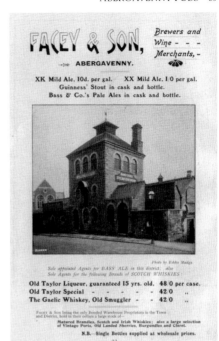

A splendid advertisement for Facey's Brewery in the Burrow's Guide *of 1903.*

between 1873 and 1875 (although Samuel Facey owned the site in 1873, it is described in the Water Rate Book as a garden). New and extended premises were built on the same site in 1892, consisting of a main stone building which contained offices, sample rooms, showrooms, salerooms and, at the rear, a 'compact brewery, fitted with plant and machinery on the tower principle ... a force of ten practical men, under experienced superintendence, is kept permanently employed'. A billhead of 1899 describes the firm as:

> Sole appointed agents and bottlers of Bass's India Pale and Burton Ales, Guinness's Stout, Old Irish and Scotch Whiskies, Nicholson's London Gin, Ports and Sherries from Best Shippers.

Facey's also ran two malthouses, one in Lion Street and the other in Mill Street, and managed the Abergavenny Bonded Stores in the basement of the Market Hall. In 1880, Samuel Facey built The Elms in Belmont Road as the family home. After Samuel Facey's death in June 1904, the business passed to his son Frank Henry, who had been a partner since 1892. On his death in 1933, his son Frank Edward Wainwright took over and expanded the company.

As early as 1873, Samuel Facey had bought the Bush Inn in Tudor Street as an outlet for his beer and in 1880 he is also recorded as the owner of the Tanner's Arms in Mill Street. By 1950, when the company was taken over by the David Roberts and Sons Ltd Brewery of Aberystwyth, the brewery owned thirteen pubs in the district: the New Market Inn, Lion Street; the Railway Hotel, Brecon Road; the White Swan Hotel, Cross Street; the Castle Stores Inn, Mill Street; the Horse and Jockey on the old road to Raglan (now the B4598); the Herbert Arms Inn (now the Charthouse) in Llanfihangel Gobion; the Red Lion Inn, Bryngwyn; the Half Moon Hotel, Llanthony; the Swan Inn and the White Hart in Crickhowell; the Royal Victoria Hotel, Blaenafon; the Holly Bush Inn, Ebbw Vale and the Cornewall Arms in Clodock.

Brewing ceased at Market Street in 1950 but the premises continued in use as a bottling store and depot. In 1957, Roberts merged with Hope and Anchor Breweries Ltd of Sheffield and B. Grant and Co. Ltd of Burton to form Facey Ltd Wholesale and Retail Beer, Wine and Spirit Merchants. The company headquarters moved to Jubilee House in Llanfoist in April 1958. The old Market Street brewery was then put up for sale.

MERTHYR ROAD

NO. 24, MERTHYR ROAD

This building was built sometime between 1834 and 1839. In that year, it is recorded as the home of Horatio Baker, as a tenant of Evan Herbert. The trade directory for 1835 lists Mr Baiker as a brewer in Nevill Street. The site of his new home in the Merthyr Road is shown quite clearly on the 1843 tithe map (plot 434).

On census night, 7 June 1841, the house was occupied by Mary Ann Baker, aged twenty, whose occupation is given as 'Innkeeper'. This is the only known record of this building in use as a public house. Also in residence were Marian (aged seven), Horatio (aged five) and William Baker (aged fourteen), who were almost certainly the brothers and sisters of Mary Ann and the children of Horatio snr.

THE LAMB INN, NO. 25, MERTHYR ROAD

(also known as the Carpenter's Arms)

Although there was a Lamb Inn in Frogmore Street in the eighteenth century, the earliest record of the Merthyr Road hostelry dates to 1835, when William Jenkins is listed as a beer retailer in the 'New road'. He is also recorded in the 1843 tithe records as occupying the cottages and gardens where the Lamb stood, as a tenant of Baker Gabb.

By May 1850, with John Jenkins as owner and landlord, the pub was known as the Carpenter's Arms. By June 1851, the name had reverted to the Lamb and the landlord was Richard South. At that time the street was called the Merthyr New Road. Among the papers in the Abergavenny Museum is a small ticket with the following advertisement:

To Be Disposed of

(By Way of Chance)

A

Double-Case Watch,

At the Lamb Inn,

On Saturday, June 21st, 1884.

Tickets, Sixpence Each.

This was obviously an early form of raffle designed to draw extra custom to the house.

Publicans: William Jenkins (1835-1843), John Jenkins (1850), Richard South (June 1851-1876), Henry John Morgan (1884), Walter Robert Taylor (1891-1906), William Matthews (1910-June 1914), William Williams (1923-1926), John Henry Watkins (1934-15 November 1938), William Williams (15 November 1938-1939).

Owners (when known): John Jenkins (1850-1853), Mrs Wheeley (1859-1873), Louisa Mary Bannerman (1914), Hancock & Co. Brewers (1938-1939).

THE SOMERSET ARMS INN, NO. 62, MERTHYR ROAD

(formerly the Somerset Inn)

Originally known as the Somerset Inn, the pub is first recorded in 1841, though we do not know the name of the publican, Rachel Price, until 1862.

By 1901, the pub had expanded to include No. 66, Merthyr Road. Always popular with railwaymen, the Somerset is recorded in 1901 as the headquarters of the Abergavenny branch of the Amalgamated Society of Railway Servants (Enoch R. Evans, sec.). The pub also ran large charabanc tours for its regulars in the early years of the twentieth century.

For many years, beer was brewed on the premises and the remains of the brewhouse can be seen at the rear of the building. The house was still known as the Somerset Inn in 1914.

Publicans: Rachel Price (1862), John Millett (1865), Thomas Jones (1868), James Williams (1871), Thomas James (1872-1873), Edgar Monks (1876), Thomas James (1877), Francis William Hambling (1880-1884), Mrs Catherine F. Powell (1891-1906) William Creese (1910-1912), James N. Ellis (May 1914), Mrs Mary A. James (June 1914), listed but publican not named (1921-1938), M. Tutt (until 14 June 1938), D.E. Thomas (15 June 1938-1939).

Owners (when known): Mrs Powell (1859), J. Powell (1860), Mrs S. Powell (1868-1872), J.H. Morgan (1873), Thomas Alexander Webb (1914), Arnold Perret & Co. Brewers (1938).

THE WHITE LION, NOS 106-114, MERTHYR ROAD

This row of cottages was built sometime between 1834 and 1839. In 1839, Richard Adams is recorded as occupying two fields and a house, garden and stabling known as the White Lion. This is the only known record of this particular pub. The site is shown quite clearly on the 1843-1844 tithe map and Richard Adams was still the occupier at that time.

Publicans: Richard Adams (1839).
Owners: Thomas Price (1839).

The Somerset Inn, 1920s. These gentlemen may be the Amalgamated Society of Railway Servants on their annual outing.

MILL STREET

Until the summer of 1859, all of what is now Cross Street below the Coach and Horses was part of Mill Street. This can cause some confusion, as buildings we would now think of as being in Cross Street are recorded in nineteenth-century documents as standing in Mill Street.

THE EARL GREY INN, NO. 24, CROSS STREET
Until 1859, this building, which was probably built around 1800, was the first house in Mill Street. It is recorded as a beerhouse in 1835 and is first called the Earl Grey Inn in 1839. Both the known landlords had other trades: Richard Whistance was a baker and flour dealer and John Williams is described in the 1851 census as a 'Master Saddler'. The pub had certainly closed by 1858 and was then run as a grocer's or baker's shop by Miss Hannah Lockley.

The Earl Grey referred to in the pub name was a popular Whig statesman in the early years of the nineteenth century. He was first Lord of the Admiralty during the Napoleonic Wars and, as Prime Minister, was responsible for the passing of the great Reform Act of 1832. In boroughs such as Abergavenny, this gave the right to vote to all men who occupied property rated at £10 or more a year. The effect was to give the vote to the middle classes.

Publicans: Richard Whistance (1835-1844), John Williams (1850-1852), ? Powell (1856).
Owners (when known): Richard Whistance (1839-1851), William Parry (1856).

THE BOAR'S HEAD, NO 31, CROSS STREET
Although the current building dates only from 1877, it stands on the site of Boar's Head Yard, named after the pub which once stood here and which is recorded in 1787 and 1791. To commemorate this fact, there is a carved boar's head above the archway of one of the passages leading through the building. By the 1850s, Boar's Head Yard was a centre of Abergavenny's flourishing shoemaking industry.

Publicans: Mr Mathews (1787), John Harris (1791).

THE TANNER'S ARMS, NO. 7, MILL STREET
This house is first recorded in 1868, when it is simply listed as a beerhouse with Thomas Gardner as the landlord. It is first called the Tanner's Arms in 1873. In 1880, Samuel Henry Facey, the local brewer (*see* Market Street), agreed to sell the pub 'called or known by the name of the "Tanner's Arms" now in the occupation of Thomas Gardner' to Richard Baker Gabb for the sum of £430. It is not known whether the sale went ahead as planned, for in the same year Thomas Gardner is recorded as the pub's owner as well as publican. The names of the landlords are not recorded after 1910 and the pub had closed by May 1914.

Publicans: Thomas Gardner (1868-1880), Thomas Moses (1884-1910).
Owners (when known): F. Williams (1868), Mrs Bevan (1872), C. Bevan (1873), Samuel Henry Facey (1880), Richard Baker Gabb (1880), Thomas Gardner (1880), Facey & Son (1914).

THE BLACK HORSE, NO. 8, MILL STREET
This beerhouse is first recorded in 1839, with Richard James as landlord. It is only referred to once as the Black Horse, in 1852. There had formerly been another Black Horse on the site now covered by

Nos 27-28 Cross Street (then also part of Mill Street). This seems to have closed before 1822 but we know the names of two of its publicans: Ann Alcheson, widow, and John Williams. This may be the 'John Williams, Innholder' recorded on a survey of St Mary's churchyard as having died in 1822.

Publicans: Ann Alcheson and John Williams (pre-1822), Richard James (1839-1853).
Owners (when known): Henrietta Jones (1839-1853).

THE CASTLE STORES INN, NO. 29, MILL STREET
(formerly the Three Tuns Inn)

Formerly known as the Three Tuns, this pub stood on the south side of the steps that now lead from Mill Street up to the Castle Walk. The building itself dated to 1680-1700 and originally served as the town's poorhouse. The first record of its use as a pub dates to 1787, when it was run by the Widow Cadogan. On 19 December 1794, the Abergavenny Improvement Commissioners resolved 'to purchase the Three Tuns, previously used as a poor-house in Mill Street, of Mrs Morgan, widow, and Mr Thomas, surgeon, for the sum of £330'.

In 1805, the pub was bought by Robert Smith of Abergavenny, victualler, from Mary Jones of the Hendre, Usk. On 6 September 1815, the Commissioners granted a certificate to Thomas Newman for a licence on the premises.

Mill Street, c. 1968. The old Black Horse is second from the left in this row of cottages with dormer windows.

The Castle Stores Inn in 1912.

In 1852, publican Joseph Denner is described as a victualler and baker. Despite being renamed the Castle Stores Inn sometime between 1862 and 1864, the pub was still known locally as the Tuns well into the twentieth century. For a brief period in 1873 and 1874, the name actually reverted to the Three Tuns Inn. In June 1874, the pub was bought for £500 by the Right Honourable Fathome Hardy MP and the Right Honourable Ralph Pelham Nevill. Between 1884 and 1891, the premises were kept by Sidney Morgan, the Town Crier. He was succeeded as publican by his son, Thomas Peter Morgan. By 1938, the pub had been taken over by Facey's Brewery and became one of their tied houses (*see* Market Street).

Publicans: Widow Cadogan (1787), Elizabeth Cadogan (1791), Widow Morgan and Mr Thomas, surgeon (1794), Thomas Newman (1815), Thomas Bath (1822-1830), William Davies (1835), William Trew (1839-1842), Thomas Coward (1850), John Richards (May 1850), James Moore (1851), Joseph Denner (1852-1853), Henry Edwards (1858-1859), Henry Edworthy (1860), Thomas Richards (1862), M.A. Goodwin (1864), Thomas Richards (1865-1868), William Bettridge (1871), Jeremiah Jones (1873-1877), Sidney Morgan (1884-1895), Thomas Peter Morgan (1901-1910), Arthur Price (1914-1923), William Ritchings (1926), Ernest Richard Edwards (1934-1939).
Owners (when known): Widow Morgan and Mr Thomas, surgeon (1794), Robert Smith (1805-1840), Mrs Smith (1850-1851), Elizabeth Smith (1853), William Hughes (1859), Mrs Hughes (1860-1873), Rt Hon. Fathome Hardy MP and Rt Hon. Ralph Pelham Nevill (1874), Marquis of Abergavenny (1914), Facey & Son Brewers (1938).

THE UNICORN INN, NO. 36, MILL STREET
The Unicorn stood on the western side of the street near the Mill Street bridge over the River Gavenny. It was a seventeenth-century building with a very fine old dog-leg staircase in oak. It had high ceilings with Tudor rose and pineapple designs. The rear walls were 30in thick, while the front walls were of lath and plaster with heavy oak timber-framing. The overflow from the old millrace ran at the back into the Gavenny and often caused flooding of the pub cellars.

   The earliest recorded publican is George Williams in 1815, though there is some evidence that the family had been in possession of the pub since at least the mid-1780s. One of their descendants, Samuel Williams, emigrated to America in the 1850s and wrote a memoir which included reference to the Unicorn:

   The old homestead in Abergavenny where my father [Edward] was born, was called 'The Unicorn', a public house which belonged to the family a great many years... After being in the navy twelve or fourteen years, he came home to England and was in Exeter recruiting, when he met my mother [Elizabeth] and married her.

   Almost immediately he returned to his old home in Wales taking his wife with him. He found his mother dead, and everything that was possible to move had been taken by his sister whom he never forgave.

Unfortunately, there are no specific dates given for any of the events described, except for Edward's marriage to Elizabeth, which took place in 1814. If he had joined the navy between sixteen and eighteen years of age, he would have been born between 1782 and 1784. From 1815 on, the pub was home to a Society of Tradesmen and Gentlemen. By 1830, the pub was being run by George Williams' wife, Elizabeth. In September 1832, a women's friendly society which had previously been based at

No. 36, Mill Street, the old Unicorn Inn.

the New Swan moved to the Unicorn. It was still going strong in 1838. Writing around 1880, 'an Abergavenny Octogenarian' recalled that in his youth:

> The Unicorn Inn, being then in one of the principal streets in the town – Lower Mill-street – which was then the only entrance into the town from Monmouth, Caerleon and Newport, was one of the best public-houses in the town, but it lost a great portion of its custom when the new portion of the road from the Swan to Pen-y-Cawse was constructed.

This New Road (as it was briefly called) was built in 1847. In September 1850, the Women's Benefit Society was on the move again, this time to the King's Head in Cross Street. In his will, dated 5 November 1854, James Morgan 'of the Unicorn, Abergavenny, Innkeeper', left all his estate 'to my dear wife'.

In the period around 1906, the licensee of the pub was James Rogers but the pub was mostly run by his wife Priscilla and their elder daughters, Lillian and May. In 1977, their youngest daughter, Laura, published a memoir of her life, entitled *Life's Revolving Gate*, which includes her memories of life in the Unicorn:

> A three storey house, with five bedrooms, a private sitting room and kitchen, two lounge rooms and bar. The pub was run by my mother and two sisters, with help from my father at weekends and bank

holidays ... market day was a busy one, there were so many country folk calling. One little old man came regularly asking if he could put his horse in one of the stables and leave his trap too. He was a maker of beesoms and sold them in the market amongst other things, always giving mother a beesom to sweep the paths and leaves.

Two regular visitors at bank holiday times were a violinist and his wife, for whom a bedroom was prepared. They played the violin and cello to the delight of the customers. Minnie and I would sit on the stairs and listen, we were never allowed into the public rooms... As time went on it was decided there were too many public houses in a small area and two of them had to be closed and the licensees compensated. The Unicorn was one of them, which was a great relief to my mother, and we were able to leave and reside at Alexandra Road.

The pub had certainly closed by June 1912, for by that time James and Priscilla Rogers were living in Laburnum House in Monk Street. Despite this, it is still listed in the Abergavenny trade directories (with no licensees named) until 1921.

Publicans: Williams family (from around 1782-1784 onwards), George Williams (1815-1822), Elizabeth Williams (1830-1842), James Hardman (1850-1852), James Morgan (1853-1854), W and C. Dale (1856), Charles Dale (1858-1859), William Roberts (1862-1864), James Roberts (1865), ? Roberts (1868), William Roberts (1871-1884), Thomas Nicholls (1891), Joseph Jones (1895-1901), James Rogers (1906), listed 1912-1921.
Owners (when known): James Jones (1839-1868), Misses Jones (1873), J.W. Prosser (1914).

The Unicorn's fine seventeenth-century staircase.

THE TWO REFORMERS INN, NO. 59, MILL STREET

From a comparison of the 1850 Poor Rate Book with Wood's map of Abergavenny of 1834, it seems likely that this pub occupied No. 59, Mill Street. The earliest record of the place dates to 1835, when it was run by John Prosser. It is first called the Two Reformers Inn in 1839. The name of the landlady, Ann Prosser, is crossed out in the Rate Book for May 1850, so it is possible that she had left by then. The pub had closed by 1853 and in the 1873 Water Rate Book is described as being in ruins.

The 'Two Reformers' were Earl Grey (1764-1845) and Lord John Russell (1792-1878), the statesmen responsible for the passing of the great Reform Act of 1832 (*see* the Earl Grey Inn).

Publicans: John Prosser (1835-1839), Ann Prosser (1842-1850).
Owners (when known): John Rushworth (1839-1853).

Other public houses recorded in Mill Street during the nineteenth century but whose exact whereabouts are not known were:

THE NEW INN

This pub is only recorded between 1822 and 1825. A handbill preserved in the museum informs the public that 'Two Very Capital Stage Waggons' were to be sold by auction 'at the New Inn in the town of Abergavenny' on Friday 13 May 1825.

Publicans: J. Lewis (1822-1823).

THE MASON'S ARMS

This pub is only recorded once by name, in 1852. From the 1853 Poor Rate Book, where Thomas Price is listed as a shopkeeper, it would seem that the house stood somewhere near what is now the corner of Mill Street and Cross Street. Thomas Price is still recorded as a 'beerhouse keeper' in 1857. The other Mason's Arms (on Hereford Road) had changed its name to the Victoria Inn by 1850.

Publicans: Thomas Price (1852-1857).

THE ANGLER'S ARMS

(formerly the Cantreff Arms)

This pub stood at the very end of Mill Street, near Monmouth Road. It is only recorded twice: as the Cantreff Arms in 1859, with John Pugh as publican, and as the Angler's Arms in the 1860 Street and Water Rate Book, where the then publican, Thomas Pugh, is described as insolvent. At that time, it was one of the string of pubs owned by William Morgan of the Phoenix Brewery in Lion Street.

It seems possible that the pub was rebuilt by William Cooper sometime between 1860 and 1865 and renamed the Belle Vue Hotel (*see* Monmouth Road), though the evidence for this is far from conclusive.

Publicans: John Pugh (1859), Thomas Pugh (1860).
Owners (when known): ? Griffiths (1859), William Morgan (1860).

BEERHOUSES

Various beerhouse keepers are recorded in Mill Street at various times during the nineteenth century but the exact location of their houses are unknown: John Cawthorn (1835), James Weager (1842-1844), William Crates (1850), William Jones (1850).

MONK STREET

THE GATE HOUSE, ST MARY'S CHAMBERS
(formerly the King's Arms)
This beerhouse is first recorded in 1835, with William Watkins as publican. It is only referred to once as the King's Arms, in 1839. In 1852, it is called the Gate House. It seems to have closed for a brief period in 1860 and is last recorded as a beerhouse in July 1872.

Publicans: William Watkins (1835-1844), Benjamin Whistance (1850), John Wheeler (1851-1852), William Thayer (1853), David Williams (1856-1864), Phillip Pritchard (1865-1868), William Cole (1871-1872).
Owners (when known): Charles Kemys Tynte Esq. (1839), Joseph Cole (1850-1859), Mrs Cole (1860-1864), ? Cole (1868), William Cole (1872).

THE NEW FOUNTAIN, NO. 12, MONK STREET
The first reference to this house dates to 1868, when it was a beerhouse kept by David Williams. It is first referred to as the New Fountain in 1876. Between 1877 and 1884, the pub was run by George Bull, who also doubled as a barber – he is listed as 'a hairdresser and beer retailer'. By 1901, the premises had been converted into a tobacconist's shop.

Publicans: David Williams (1868-1871), William Williams (1873), Mrs Alice Williams (1875-1877; M. Williams also recorded in 1876), George Bull (1877-1884), Thomas Davies (1891).
Owners (when known): Jeremiah Francomb (1868), 'Estate of the late J. Francomb' (1873).

THE NAG'S HEAD, NO. 21, MONK STREET
(also known as the Ale Stores)
The Nag's Head was an old thatched building that stood on the site later covered by the Pavilion cinema (now the Gateway Christian Centre). It was certainly in business in 1784, as its pub sign can be clearly seen in a small watercolour by Joshua Gosselin painted in July of that year. However, the first recorded publican is Ann Morgan in 1791.

In 1873, the pub is called the Ale Stores. By this time, the place was owned by Charles Tucker, who also owned the Great George and a wine merchant's business at No. 10, Cross Street (*see* the Borough Arms). In 1880, it is again referred to as the Nag's Head. From 1884 until 1923, the place housed a coach-building works.

Publicans: Ann Morgan (1791), Henry Phillips (1822), Elizabeth Phillips (1830), Richard Whitcomb (1835-died 1841), Elizabeth Whitcomb (1842), Richard Shaw (1850-1853), Ellen Follett (1856-1860), Edwin Holtham (1862-1865), William Jones (1868-1871), Isaac Isaacs (1872), Charles Tucker (1873-1880).

Monk Street in July 1784, from a watercolour by Joshua Gosselin (1739-1813). The thatched cottage on the left is the old Nag's Head Inn; the pub sign can be clearly seen. This building was demolished shortly after 1896 to make way for a carriage works and the site was later occupied by the Pavilion cinema, now the Gateway Christian Centre.

Owners (when known): Charles Kemys Tynte Esq. (1839-1840), Morris Jenkins (1850-1851), Richard Shaw (1853-1860), Isaac Isaacs (1864-1872), Charles Tucker (1873-1880).

THE LONDON HOTEL, NO. 23, MONK STREET
(formerly the London Apprentice Inn)

The original name of this pub was derived from a popular eighteenth-century ballad that recounted a London apprentice's countless adventures in the far-flung corners of the globe, which included robbing 'the lion of his heart'. The apprentice was usually shown on pub signs with a lion's heart in each hand.

The pub's first recorded publican is a Mr Herbert in 1787. By 1791, the publican was Mary Herbert. In 1808, the pub was the venue for meetings of a Society of Tradesmen and Gentlemen Farmers. In the early nineteenth century, bull-baiting used to take place on the crossroads outside the pub. This must have been awkward because, in the period around 1817, the magistrates' court was also held in the pub.

By 1835, the publican was Thomas Herbert and in 1837 the pub was the headquarters of the London Women's Friendly Society, which was still active in 1852. Thomas Herbert died in 1848 and by 1851 the publican was William Trew, a butcher who had married Thomas's daughter Elizabeth. In 1860, the pub's rateable value stood at £47 10s. At that time, William Trew also owned the Bridge End Inn on Monmouth Road and ran the Clarence Inn in Castle Street. By 1865, Edward Lewis had taken over as publican. Mrs Trew is still recorded as the owner in 1868.

In 1873, the pub is referred to as the London Hotel for the first time and is valued at £51 5s. At that time, Thomas Evans was both publican and owner and it may well have been he who changed the name. In a petition to the Abergavenny Improvement Commissioners signed by the publican, Richard John, in 1876, the pub is again referred to as the London Hotel. The petition was for the opening of the cattle market gate on market day 'for the convenience of taking in the Cattle, and to prevent overcrowding'. As Thomas Evans is still listed as the publican in 1877, it is likely that Richard John was a tenant.

For a brief period around 1884, the premises were known as the London Temperance Hotel. It was back in business as a pub by 1891, with John Dale as publican. In the late nineteenth century, the local

The London Hotel in 1967.

nickname for the house was the Bell-ringer's Arms, as the St Mary's bell-ringers met there so often. By 1914, the pub had been bought up by the Rhymney Brewery and became one of their tied houses. The building was converted into flats in 1978.

Publicans: Mr Herbert (1787), Mary Herbert (1791), Richard Morgan (1822-1830), Thomas Herbert (1835-died 1848), Mrs Herbert (May 1850), Elizabeth Herbert (1850), William Trew (1851-1864), Edward Lewis (1865-1868), Thomas Evans (1871-1875), Richard John (1876-1877), Thomas Evans (1877), John Shadrach (1880), Miss Harriet Tims (1884, as London Temperance Hotel), Samuel Davies (sometime between 1885-1890), John Harris Dale (1891, as London Hotel), James Price (1895), Albert Price (1901), Miss Margaret Jane Jenkins (1906), John Ethelbert Taylor (1910-1921), Charles Wadelin (1923-1926), Tom Osmond Evans (1934-1939).
Owners (when known): Thomas Herbert (1839-1840), Mrs Herbert (1850), Mrs Trew (1851), William Trew (1853-1864), Mrs Elizabeth Trew *née* Herbert (1868), Thomas Evans (1872-1873), Rhymney Brewery Co. Ltd (1914-1938).

THE COUNTY CLUB, NO. 2, LOWER MONK STREET
This building dates back to the eighteenth century and was originally the mansion of the Roberts family. They were wealthy local landowners in the eighteenth and early nineteenth centuries and there are fine wall monuments to them in St Mary's. In 1890, the premises were sold to the County Club. The club was still there in 1939. Later, the building became part of the Monmouthshire Constabulary headquarters.

THE OMAR PASHA, NO. 13, LOWER MONK STREET
Although this large building dates from around 1600, it is first recorded as a beerhouse in 1842, with a Mary Probert as publican. The earliest reference to the house as the Omar Pasha (then spelt 'Omar Pacha') dates to 1860. Omar Pasha (1806-1871) was an Austrian (his real name was Michael Lattas) who became a general in the Turkish army and achieved great success and fame during the Crimean War (1854-1856) when Britain, France and Turkey fought against Russia. He later became the Turkish minister of war.

On 4 May 1872, the following report appeared in the *Abergavenny Chronicle*:

> Elizabeth W-----, who did not appear, was charged with being drunk at 10-30 p.m., on Saturday night last in Ireland-street, and enticing men across from the Omar Pasha beerhouse into a brothel. After she had taken one man to the brothel, she came and fetched another one who declined her kind invitation. – Sergeant Edghill told her to desist, which she did – Fined 10s. including costs or 7 days.

In July of the same year, Thomas Hubball – described as an 'old offender' – was charged with being drunk and disorderly in Monk Street:

> The constable stated that defendant challenged the landlord of the Omar Pasha [Charles Beams] to fight because he would not supply him with drink – Fined 21s, including costs, or one month.

Publicans: Mary Probert (1842-1844), Edward Lewis (1850), Thomas Hoskins (1851), Thomas Denning (1853), Charles Beams (1856-1872), Joseph Thomas (1873).
Owners (when known): Charles Kemys Tynte Esq. with John Probert as tenant (1839), Elizabeth Probert (1850-1851), late John Probert (1853-1860), 'late Probert' (1864), Mr C. Cheese (1868-1872), Joseph Thomas (1873).

THE GLOBE, NO. 14, LOWER MONK STREET
Confusingly, there were two Globes in Abergavenny in 1852, John Lloyd's in Monk Street and the house run by John Morgan Edmonds in Castle Street (though this became the Castle Inn in June 1852). John Lloyd is still listed as living in Monk Street in the 1853 Rate Book. The Globe stood on the northern side of the street, four doors down from the Dog Inn, later the site of No. 14, Lower Monk Street.

Publicans: John Lloyd (1852).

Other public houses listed in Monk Street but whose exact whereabouts are unknown, include:

THE STAR
A document in the museum collections dated to 1858 records Emma Saranger as the licensee of the 'Star Public House' in Monk Street, though its exact whereabouts are unknown.

BEERHOUSES
A house and garden owned by Thomas Goode stood somewhere near the junction of Monk Street and Hereford Road. At different times, it is listed under Monk Street, Ireland Street, New Hereford Road and Hereford Road. It is only recorded as a beerhouse in 1850 and 1851. The earliest recorded publican is John Morgan Edmunds in 1850.

Publicans: John Morgan Edmunds (May 1850), Mrs Bowcott (June 1851).
Owners: Thomas Goode (May 1850-1873).

Other beer retailers are recorded in Monk Street but the exact locations of their houses are not known:

Ann Pritchard (1850), William Rosser (1850), Benjamin Whistone (1850; probably the Benjamin

Whistance of the King's Arms above), ? Bath (1864), Thomas Richards (1865), Thomas White (1865), Ellen Williams (1865).

BREWERIES (LOCATIONS UNKNOWN)

John Brock (later of the Market House Tavern) is recorded in the St Mary's parish registers as a brewer in Monk Street in July 1830. We do not know the exact whereabouts of his brewery and by 1832 he had moved to Lion Lane. Delabere Walker is named as a brewer in Monk Street in 1852. Again, the exact whereabouts of his brewery are not known.

PORTER DEALERS

John Cadogan is listed as a porter merchant between 1835 and 1852. The 1852 trade directory describes him as an 'ale, porter and timber merchant'. His warehouse stood next door to the Great George and was owned by Revd R.W.P. Davies. In 1853, it was occupied by Mrs Cadogan and it is possible that John Cadogan had died in 1852 or 1853. In January 1864, it is listed as a beerhouse occupied by William Cowles.

Thomas Richards traded as porter dealer from the Tithe Barn from 1835 to 1844. The business had moved to No. 52, Castle Street by 1850, where Richards is recorded until 1859.

MONMOUTH ROAD

THE ABERGAVENNY HOTEL

(formerly the Belle Vue Hotel and the Rothesay Hotel)

It is possible that this pub started life as the Cantreff Arms (later the Angler's Arms; *see* Mill Street). The earliest reference to the Belle Vue Hotel dates to 1865, with William Cooper as publican. He also owned the premises. In 1880, even though William Cooper still owned and lived in the pub, it was being run by William Gardiner (or Gardner) as his tenant. The house is first referred to as the Rothesay Hotel in 1891. By the 1920s, the hotel had been bought up by Hancock's Brewery and was being run as tied house with tenant landlords.

The Rothesay Hotel (Abergavenny Hotel) sometime in the 1920s or 1930s.

Publicans: William Cooper (1865-1877), William Gardiner (1880-1884), Mrs Mary Sampson (1891), Daniel Probett (1895), James Samuel (1901), Miss Jane Edmunds (1906-1912), Edwin Herbert Attwood (1914), Mrs Frederick Williams (1923), Thomas Morris (December 1923-August 1926), Mrs Mabel Morris (August 1926-February 1936), Mrs Elsie May Hall (February-May 1936), Francis Thomas (1937-1939).

Owners (when known): William Cooper (1868-1880), John Owen Marsh (1914), Hancock & Co. Brewers (1938-1939).

THE BRIDGE END INN, NO. 17, MONMOUTH ROAD

The Bridge End occupied the row of houses between the Abergavenny Hotel and the bridge over the River Gavenny. It is first mentioned in 1853, with William Cooper as publican. By 1865, he had bought the nearby Belle Vue Hotel.

In his will, dated 13 August 1872, the then owner John Astbury (who ran a china shop in Market Street) left the pub to his mother, Sarah Simcocks, and to his friends, grocer William Price and printer Henry Thomas. His sister, Ellen Myatt, was to receive the rents and profits of the premises for the term of her natural life. John Astbury died on 16 August. However, the will was contested and the case dragged on in the Court of Chancery until the 1890s, by which time most of those originally involved had died.

For a period in the 1870s, Ellen Myatt's husband Joseph ran the pub. He later took over his brother-in-law's old china shop in Market Street. Ellen Myatt died intestate on 12 August 1890.

In February 1897, Mrs Sarah Mitcheson sold the pub to Charles Edwards, the Llanfoist brewer, for £1,175. At that time, the tenant was James Williams and his annual rent stood at £35.

The last recorded landlord is William Joseph Brooks in 1934. The pub is not recorded in the 1938 Rate Book and, by 1939, the building was known as Bridge Cottages.

Publicans: William Cooper (1853-1864), William Trew (1865), Miss Elizabeth Miller (1871), Misses Miller (1872), Joseph Myatt (1873-1877), David Edwards (1880), James Hunt (1884), Mrs Lucy Elizabeth Hunt (1891), Joseph Williams (1895), James Williams (1897), Mrs Emma Poole (1901), George Rosser (1906-1910), Raymond John Hook (1914-1923), Henry Thomas (1926), William Joseph Brooks (1934).

Owners (when known): Edwin Baugh (1853), William Trew (1856-1865), John Astbury (1872), Sarah Simcocks, William Price and Henry Thomas (1872), William Watkins (1872-1873), Mrs Sarah Mitcheson (1897), Charles Edwards Brewery Ltd (1897-1914).

THE BELMONT INN, NO. 22, MONMOUTH ROAD

(formerly the Blorenge Inn)

This pub started life as a beerhouse and is first recorded in 1862. In 1865, John Powell, the publican, is described as a beer retailer and coal dealer. By 1867, the pub was known as the Blorenge Inn and was one of the many houses owned by William Morgan of the Phoenix Brewery in Lion Street. William Morgan the Younger had been living at Pen y Causeway (now called The Elms) behind the pub since at least 1847.

In October 1883, John Powell moved from the Blorenge and took out a 7-year lease on the Wellington Inn in Cross Street. The house is first listed as the Belmont Inn in 1891.

Publicans: John Powell (1862), William Thomas (1864), John Powell (1865-October 1883), Alfred Luke Powell (1891-1906), Charles Morgan (1910-1921), William Henry Davies (1923-1926), Arthur E. Walters (1934), Harry Vincent Davies (1937-1938), F. Thomas (1939).

Owners (when known): ? Griffiths (1864), William Morgan (1868), John Owen Marsh (1914), Hancock & Co. Brewers (1938-1939).

BEERHOUSES (LOCATIONS UNKNOWN)
Thomas Price (1858).

NEVILL STREET

The earliest known innholders in Nevill Street are John Lewis and Mathew Price, named in the former's will dated 6 May 1686. Unfortunately, the exact whereabouts of their premises are not known. By the terms of his will, John Lewis bequeathed 'unto my loveing kinsman and friend Edward Lewis ... my messuage or tenement wherein Mathew Price vitler now doth inhabite'. The full inventory of John Lewis's goods 'att the time of his demise, taken and appraized ... upon the 12th day of May in the year of our Lord 1686' includes:

Item in drink & sider in the Cellar 60   3:0:0
Item wooden vatts trinds hogsheads & other wooden vessells of all sorts   2:10:0
Item in ready made malt; and malt upon the floores in making   15:0:0

THE RAVEN HOTEL, NOS 1-3, NEVILL STREET
The rear of the present building is considerably older than the frontage. In a deed of 1810, the building is described as 'a Dwelling House called the Raven now or late in the respective occupation of William Griffiths, tailor, and Henry and John Valentine, shoemakers'. By July 1826, the building had become known as Waterloo House and was a draper's shop run by 'W. Jennings ... at much lower prices than any other Shop in this part of the County'.

It is not recorded as a pub again until 1862, when it is listed in the trade directory as the Raven Hotel, with Henry Thompson as publican. By 1865, the premises had been taken over for use as a surgery by Samuel Steele, physician. From 1884 until 1947, the building was the home of Cadle's Grocery. According to the present occupants, the front part of the building was used as a bar and until quite recently the wire cages on the front of the bottle racks were still in position in the vaulted cellars.

The Raven is not common as a pub name and is thought to be a Jacobite symbol of loyalty to the Stuarts. It is interesting to recall that Abergavenny lost its borough charter in 1689 when the town bailiff (mayor) refused to swear allegiance to William of Orange, who had been brought in by Parliament to replace the Stuart King James II.

Publicans: Henry Thompson (1862).

THE KING'S HEAD, NO. 7, NEVILL STREET
The earliest record of this King's Head is a lease dated 20 June 1712, which records that John Hanbury Esq. of Pontypool leased the property 'to be held during the three natural lives of Joshua James, Thomas James his son and Mary James his daughter' at an annual rent of £5.

In 1735, John Hanbury leased the pub again, this time to William Waters of Abergavenny, gentleman. The tenants at that time were Jehosophat Jones and his wife, Mary – the Mary James mentioned in the lease of 1712.

In December 1754, the house was in the occupation of Francis Lewis, clerk. In September 1757, the ownership of the pub passed to Thomas Roberts, a tanner from Newnham in Gloucestershire, as William Waters was unable to pay the balance of a mortgage that he had taken out in 1744. This is the last mention of the building as a pub.

Publicans: Joshua James (1712), Jehosophat and Mary Jones *née* James (1735), Francis Lewis (1754).
Owners (when known): John Hanbury (1712-1735), William Waters (1757), Thomas Roberts (1757).

THE DRAGON'S HEAD INN, NOS 10-12, NEVILL STREET
(The Royal British Legion Club)

The earliest mention of the Dragon's Head is found in a letter dated 13 July 1775, addressed to a James Lewis with the instruction that it is 'to be left at the Dragon's Head, Abergavenny'. Another document, dated 21 December 1787, records that John Powell of Abergavenny sold the pub to James Watkins of Llantilio Pertholey. It describes the place as 'All that messuage in Rother Street wherein William Chambers, inn holder, and then Thomas Williams, lived and now James Davies'.

In 1787, the publican was a Mr Morgan – probably the John Morgan recorded in the 1791 *Universal British Directory*. Sometime between 1792 and 1797, William Jones, a shoemaker (the son of the James Jones of the Star and Garter in Frogmore Street), demolished the old building and built two new buildings, Nos 10 and 12 Nevill Street. The new Dragon's Head occupied No. 12.

A seventeenth-century heraldic wall painting discovered during alterations at the British Legion in 1961.

In December 1825, William Jones assigned the premises to William Ellis, described as a yeoman. In 1827, he took out a lease on Wyke's new brewery in Lion Street and started his very successful career as a brewer (*see* Lion Street and Baker Street). In 1842, he married Mary, William Jones' daughter.

The Dragon's Head is last recorded in 1853. In 1910, the premises are listed as a temperance hotel under the management of Miss Florence Watkins. The building was taken over by the Royal British Legion in 1926.

Publicans: William Chambers and then Thomas Williams (pre-1787), James Davies (1787), Mr Morgan (1787), John Morgan (1791), J. Edwards (1822), William Lloyd (1830), John Jayne (1835), John Ellis (1839), William Bagnall (1842-1844), Ann Jones (1850-1851), William Watkins (1852), George Pugh (1853), Miss Florence Watkins (1910).
Owners (when known): John Powell (1787), James Watkins (1787), William Jones (1792-1801), Alice Price (1803), Thomas Leonard (1803, died 1805), William Jones (1825), William Ellis (1825-1830), James Jones (1839-1853).

JAMES JONES' BREWERY, NO. 13, NEVILL STREET
James Jones is recorded as a maltster in Nevill Street between 1822 and 1864. In 1851 and 1852, he is described as a brewer. The census returns for 1851 record that he employed eight men in this brewery. By 1868, he had died.

Between 1865 and 1871, the trade directories list William Morgan Morgan, 'currier, leather merchant and maltster', at this address. However, the Rate Book for 1868 describes the malthouse as vacant, while that for 1873 lists Charles Edwards as the occupier.

Brewers: James Jones (1822-1864), Charles Edwards (1873).
Owners: James Jones (1839-1868), 'late James Jones' (1873).

THE COW INN, NO. 14, NEVILL STREET
(formerly the Post Office)
This important building dates back to the sixteenth century and may have been built as a town house for the Vaughans of Tretower. The Elizabethan carvings about the windows include the Vaughan coat of arms, though the cow's and goat's heads on the building date to around 1780, when a major refurbishment was carried out.

The earliest known record of the use of the building as public house dates to 1787. In that year and again in 1791, the pub is also referred to as the Post Office, with Mr Edward Blashfield as publican.

William Daniel, the proprietor in 1871, doubled as a painter, plumber and glazier. Between 1873 and 1880, the place was run as the Cow Temperance Hotel and by 1901 the building was owned by James Sayce and used as dining rooms. At the same time, several rooms were rented as boarding for pupils at the Castle Street School by the headmistress, Miss Radford. The pub enjoyed a brief spell in 1912 as the Nevill Temperance Hotel. The building was later used as the headquarters of the Gentlemen's Club and, from 1937 on, it acted as the local Labour Party headquarters and club under the title of Unity House.

Publicans: Edward Blashfield (1787-1791), William Brace (1822-1835), 'Brace Jnr' (1839), Rachel Price (1842-1844), Margaret Elizabeth Morse (1850-1859), William Rowley (1860-1865), W. David

The Cow Inn, c. 1910.

(sometime between 1865 and 1868), John Watkins (1868), William Daniel (1871), ? Phillips (1872), W. Price (1873), George Kennard (1880).
Owners (when known): Walter Lewis (1850-1868), Nathaniel Cook (1872), Walter Lewis (1873).

THE BLACK-A-MOOR'S HEAD, NO. 23, NEVILL STREET
Among the deeds of this building is a document of 1774 which describes it as 'lately called the Black-a-Moor's Head in Cow Street, wherein Richard Davies did formerly dwell'. By 1816, the premises had become a bakery run by William Jones.

Publicans: Richard Davies (pre-1774).

THE PYE BULL, NO. 27, NEVILL STREET
Among the deeds of this building is a feoffment dated 18 November 1655, which records that, for the sum of £93, Roger Williams 'of the parish of Lancarvan in Glamorgan, tailor' and June, his wife, sold to William Robert 'of Abergavenny, corviser [shoemaker]' and his wife, Marie houses 'heretofore called ... The Pye Bull ... in the occupation of John Edwards, corviser, Lewis Vaughan, corviser, Griffith John, labourer, John Thomas, labourer and the said William Robert'. This is the only record of this house being used as pub.

Owners (when known): Roger Williams and June, his wife (1655), William Robert and Marie, his wife (1655).

THE KING'S ARMS INN, NO. 29, NEVILL STREET
A typical sixteenth- or early seventeenth-century building, the King's Arms displays the royal arms of Charles II (1660-1685) and it seems likely that it has been a public house since that time. The first landlord known to us by name is Edward Blashfield in 1811. He had previously kept the Cow Inn (then

known as the Post Office). At that time, the house was already called the King's Arms. The Blashfield family owned the premises until at least 1860.

In 1817, the pub was used to billet a troop of the King's and 15th Hussars, called into the district in the wake of serious rioting at Nantyglo and Tredegar in 1816. Over the fireplace in the lounge, the soldiers left a permanent reminder of their stay in the form of an inscription that reads:

Good Quartering Forever
1817
King & 15 Huzzars
Hall Troop 24

In June 1849, the women's friendly society which met at the Unicorn in Mill Street moved to the King's Arms and the publican, Joseph Brown, became their new treasurer. In May 1851, they were joined by men's friendly society.

The census returns for 1851 reveal that, on the night of the count, Joseph Brown, his wife and four children, five lodgers, three servants and two coachmen were in residence at the inn. By May 1854, they had moved to the King's Head in Cross Street.

Between January 1864 and 1914, the publican was Thomas Delafield. He had started out as a beer retailer in Tudor Street, where he is listed in 1862. By 1873, he had bought the King's Arms outright and was running his own brewery at the rear of the premises. He and his family ran several other pubs and off-licences in the town, including the Sun Inn in Cross Street and No. 71, St Helen's Road and No. 55, Union Road. From 1884 until 1914, his son, Thomas Alfred Delafield, owned the Monmouthshire House in Ross Road.

The King's Arms is reputed to be haunted by the White Lady. According to the legend, she was a serving wench who was taken advantage of by a monk who had sought refuge at the inn during a period of religious persecution. Having died in childbirth, she is said to wander the upstairs rooms searching for her child. The dastardly monk was supposedly hanged, drawn and quartered at Monmouth.

The King's Arms in 1903, complete with drays from Delafield's Brewery at the rear of the premises. The arms of Charles II on the wall were probably put up to celebrate the Restoration.

The King's Arms in the late 1950s.

Publicans: Edward Blashfield (1811), John Whitmore Blashfield (1816-1835), William Challenger (1839), Timothy Wallington (1842), Joseph Brown (June 1849-1852), George Davies (1853), Mary Ann Brock (1858-1862), Thomas Delafield (1864-1914), Sarah Delafield (1914-1919), Claude S. Atkin (1923), William Rowlands (1926), David William Fenner (1934-1939).

Owners (when known): Whitmore Blashfield (1839-died 1852), 'late W. Blashfield' (1853), W. Blashfield (1859), Mrs Blashfield (1860), E. Blashfield (1860), Edward Blashfield (1864-1872), Thomas Delafield (1873-1914), Sarah Delafield (1914-1919), Arnold Perret & Co. Brewers (1938).

BEERHOUSES

NO. 21, NEVILL STREET
This fine Elizabethan building was built in around 1550 and retains many of its original features. Charles Boucher Howells is recorded as a beer retailer and maltster at this address from 1837 until 1853. He also ran a grocer's shop in Frogmore Street.

NO. 25, NEVILL STREET
James William Jones (not the same as James Jones at No.13!) is recorded as a maltster and beer retailer at this address between 1835 and 1860. By January 1864, he had died.

The 1851 census returns record that he employed three men. The malthouse was occupied by a W. Morgan between 1868 and 1873. The house at the front was used as a milliner's, shoemaker's and leather dealer's shop until William Morris Jenkins set up as a maltster and hop merchant sometime between 1884 and 1891. He is recorded here until 1906.

BREWERS
Other Nevill Street brewers whose exact whereabouts are not known include John Hurcum in 1842 and Horatio Baker in 1835. By 1839, Horatio had moved to No. 24, Merthyr Road. In 1841, his daughter Mary Ann is recorded there as an 'Innkeeper'.

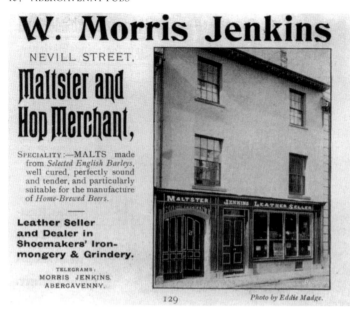

W. Morris Jenkins

NEVILL STREET,

Maltster and Hop Merchant,

SPECIALITY:—MALTS made from *Selected English Barleys*, well cured, perfectly sound and tender, and particularly suitable for the manufacture of *Home-Brewed Beers*.

Leather Seller and Dealer in Shoemakers' Ironmongery & Grindery.

TELEGRAMS:
MORRIS JENKINS,
ABERGAVENNY.

129   *Photo by Eddie Madge.*

The premises of William Morris Jenkins, maltster and hop merchant, in 1903. Between 1835 and 1860, the place was a beerhouse run by James Jones.

NEW ROAD

In the early part of the nineteenth century, several beer retailers are recorded under the address 'New Road'. Other records refer to the 'New Monmouth Road' (1828), the 'New Hereford Road' (1850) and the 'Merthyr New Road' (1852). As Princes Street (1842-1844) and the stretch of the Brecon Road from the junction with St Michael's Road to Chapel Road are also referred to as 'New Road', it is sometimes difficult to know which 'New Road' is meant.

It is possible that the William Symons listed as a beer retailer in 'New road' in 1850 is the same person as the 'William Symmonds' recorded as publican of the Cider House in Brecon Road in 1853. It is also possible that the John Jenkins also listed as a beer retailer in 'New road' in 1850 is also recorded as the owner of the Lamb Inn in 1853.

Others, the location of whose houses is not known, include Thomas Cooke (1842-1844) and William Bathurst (1852).

NORTH STREET

THE BELLE VUE, NO. 30, NORTH STREET

This beerhouse is first recorded in 1884, with Thomas Poole as publican. It is first called the Belle Vue in May 1914. In the 1938 Rate Book, it is described as an 'Off Licence – Beer Only'.

Publicans: Thomas Poole (1884), Thomas David Thomas (1891), Jacob Powell (1895-1906), Mrs Mary Thomas (1910), William Morris (1914), Miss Ida Morris (1923), William Hollings Rumsey (1926-1934), John Leslie Rumsey (1937-1939).
Owners (when known): Charles Edwards Brewery Ltd (1914-1938).

PEN Y POUND

THE HAULIER'S ARMS

David Williams is first listed as a beer retailer in Pen y Pound in 1835, though the exact location of his premises at that time is not known. The 1839 Rate Book lists two beerhouses in the Frogmore Street ward that were run by him. One stood immediately adjacent to Pen y Pound House (later St Michael's convent and now the T 'r Morwydd study centre) and was owned by a Mrs Ashe. David Williams is recorded here until 1844. The other stood next to a smithy (which later became a wheeelwright's shop) on land owned by the 'late Francis Lewis'. The site is now covered by the junction between Pen y Pound Road and Park Road. The 1834 map of Abergavenny shows a large area of land owned by Mr F. Lewis, which reached as far as the site later occupied by the King Henry VIII Grammar School (currently the Drama Centre). By 1843, the property was owned by a Jonah Clark and by 1859 by Clark and Dallow. From 1852 onwards, the beerhouse was known as the Haulier's Arms. It had certainly closed by 1873, when it is recorded as a house occupied by J.E. Evans.

Publicans: David Williams (?1835-1839), Thomas Brewer (1842-1852), Benjamin Watkins (1858-1859), Isaac Thomas (1862-1864), Ann Powell (1868-1872), S. Evan (1872).
Owners (when known): Mr F. Lewis (1834), 'late Francis Lewis' (1839), Jonah Clark (1843), 'Clark and others' (1853), Clark and Dallow (1859-1872).

PRINCES STREET

THE CARPENTER'S ARMS, NO. 1, PRINCES STREET

This house is only referred to once by this name, in 1839. The site of the house is shown on the 1843 tithe map as plot 417a. The publican was William Prosser, who is also listed as a beer retailer under

The corner of Pen y Pound and Frogmore Street in the 1960s. One of the buildings on the right is the former Haulier's Arms.

'New road' in 1842 and 1844. He was still living in the house in 1853, though not trading as a beer retailer.

Publicans: William Prosser (1839-1844).
Owners: William Prosser (1839), Baker Gabb (1843).

THE ALBERT INN, NOS 22 AND 29, PRINCES STREET
(also known as the Carpenter's Arms)
The earliest record of this pub dates to 1858, when Elizabeth Davies was the publican. It is first referred to as the Albert Inn in 1862, by which time the Prince Albert Inn in Baker Street had changed its name to the Carpenter's Arms. There seems to be some confusion about the name of the landlord in late 1860s and 1870s. He is listed in the trade directories as George Davies, but appears in the 1868 and 1873 Street and Water Rate Books as John Davies. Sometime between 1891 and 1895, either the street numbering system changed or the pub moved from No. 22 to No. 29, Princes Street. In 1914, it is listed as occupying Nos 27 and 29, Princes Street.

The last recorded landlord is William Weekes in 1926. The 1939 Rate Book describes the building as 'the Old Albert Inn, now tenements'.

Publicans: Elizabeth Davies (1858-1865), George [or 'John'] Davies (1868-1877), Frederick Spencer (1880), Thomas Howe (1884-1891), Mrs Margaret Howe (1895-1901), Austin Smart (1906), Thomas George Jones (1910), Sydney Davis (1914), Mrs Agnes Powell (1923), William Weekes (1926).
Owners (when known): Herbert George (1858-1860), Dr Franco (1864-1873), Arnold Perett & Co. Brewery (1914).

Judging the Coronation decorations in 1953. The Albert Inn is in the background on the right.

ROSS ROAD

THE MONMOUTHSHIRE HOUSE, NO. 1, ROSS ROAD
(formerly the Queen's Head and the Dog Inn)

The original pub dated from the sixteenth or early seventeenth century and, before the re-routing of the main roads into town, stood ideally placed on the corner of the highways to Monmouth and Ross-on-Wye. It was licensed to sell spirits, ale, beer, porter and cider and tobacco. Originally, ale and beer meant two entirely different things, ale being made without hops and thus producing a much sweeter brew.

The pub is first recorded in 1839 as the Queen's Head, with Philip Havard as publican. It is first referred to as the Dog Inn in 1850. At that time, Philip Havard also owned a malthouse in Monk Street, with a rateable value of £16 per annum.

Thomas Alfred Delafield held the licence from 14 February 1884 until 1915. During his ownership, the inn underwent substantial modernisation, with all but the end wall and door facing Monk Street being demolished and rebuilt. It was at this time that the pub became known as the Monmouthshire House. Mr Delafield also doubled as an insurance agent.

Later, the pub was known locally as Bailey's, after Frank Bailey, a proprietor during the 1920s and 1930s. The 1939 Rate Book records that the pub had a 'Skittle Alley and garden'. The building was demolished in 1973.

The Dog Inn in 1884.

The Monmouthshire House sometime in the 1890s.

Publicans: Phillip Havard (1839-1859), John Morgan (1860), Thomas Evans (1862-1868), Mrs Mary Prosser (1871-1884), Thomas Alfred Delafield (1884-1915), Frank Bailey (1923-1939).

Owners (when known): David Williams (1839-1840), John Morgan (1851), Philip Havard (1853-1859), John Morgan (1860), 'late P. Havard' (1864), John Morgan (1868), 'late P. Havard' (1873), Thomas Alfred Delafield (1884-1914), Cheltenham Original Brewery (1938).

BEERHOUSES
The only other beer retailer recorded in Ross Road is Joseph Robson (1842-1844). The location of his house is not known.

STATION ROAD

THE GREAT WESTERN HOTEL
(formerly the Railway Hotel, the Railway Inn, the Railway and Commercial Inn and the Great Western Railway Hotel)

The earliest record of the pub dates to 1855, when Mr Joseph Owen Marsh leased a plot of land next door. In 1858, the pub is listed under 'Taverns and Public Houses' as the Railway Inn and under 'Inns and Hotels' as the Railway and Commercial Inn. It was known as the Railway Inn in 1859 and the Railway Hotel in 1864.

The Abergavenny Bowls Club, founded in 1860, originally played on a green at the Great Western Hotel but interest waned towards the end of the nineteenth century. By 1876, the pub was known as the Great Western Railway Hotel. The current name dates from 1877. By 1914, the house was part of John Owen Marsh's public house empire. Hancock and Co. of Cardiff had acquired the pub by 1938.

The Great Western Hotel during the First World War, with the band of the 3rd Battalion, Monmouthshire Regiment drawing up in front.

Publicans: Joseph Owen Marsh (1855-1877), James Henry Howard (1880-1884), Mrs Eliza Peers (1891), Gaskell & Howell (1895), Mrs Elizabeth Julia Oliver (1901), William Evans (1906), George Mellison (1910), Harry Franklin Hardeman (1914), Charles King (1923-1939).

Owners (when known): Joseph Owen Marsh (1855-1877), James Henry Howard (1880), John Owen Marsh (1914), Hancock & Co. Brewers (1938).

ST HELEN'S ROAD

NO. 71, ST HELEN'S ROAD

For many years, this building housed a small off-licence. It was originally the property of Thomas Alfred Delafield, landlord of the Monmouthshire House, but the Hereford and Tredegar Brewing Co. bought the premises in 1919 for £750. The following information was supplied by Mr M.O. Roberts, whose parents ran the business for many years:

> These properties were built in 1877. The pre-1907 occupants were people named Jones. O. and E. Roberts [Mr Roberts' parents] were there from 1907 until 1935 followed by a Mr and Mrs Clark from Clehonger, Herefordshire and in turn by Mr and Mrs D. Matthews and lastly by Mr and Mrs R. Probert.

Further information about the occupants can be gleaned from the trade directories:

> William Joseph Oakley (1884-1895), William Edwards (1901), Thomas George Jones (1906), Owen Roberts (1907-1935), Percy Rowland Clarke (1937), D.A.T. Matthews (1938).

Owners (when known): Thomas Alfred Delafield (1914-1919), Hereford and Tredegar Brewery Ltd (1919-1938).

ST JOHN'S SQUARE

THE VINE TREE, ST JOHN'S SQUARE

The earliest recorded publican of the Vine Tree is Elizabeth Thomas in 1835. By 1839, John Hockey had taken over as publican but the pub was owned by William Ellis, the local brewer.

Before the demolition of a substantial part of St John's Square in 1958, a small alley led through the Vine Tree from St John's Square into Chicken Street and St John's Street. As a consequence, the pub was variously listed in nineteenth-century trade directories as being in St John's Square, Chicken Street and St John's Lane. In 1902, publican Frederick William Walters doubled as a carpenter and undertaker.

Mr M.O. Roberts recalls that Mr Howells, the landlord in the 1930s, 'ran a sideline selling Keynock Polish and other household cleaning requisites. He transported his wares by bicycle fitted with a carrier.'

The pub was taken over by Whitbread in 1966 and is now known as Grasshopper's.

Publicans: Elizabeth Thomas (1835), John Hockey (1839-1844), Ann Maria Prosser (1850), Watkin Prosser (1851), Robert Purslow (1852-1853), William Meredith (1859), Mrs Meredith (1860), Mrs

St John's Square in the late 1950s.

The Vine Tree and the Bull Inn in 1933.

The same view in 1957.

Rachel Kennedy (1862), William Morse (1865-1877), Mrs Mary Morse (1884), Frederick William Walters (1891-1902), Mrs Janet Ann Walters (1906), Mrs Janet Ann Harries (1910), Cornelius Harries (1914), David Jones (1923), Albert James (1926), Evan Charles Howells (1934), Tom Tomlin (1937-1939).

Owners (when known): William Ellis (1839-June 1851), John P. Williams (July 1851-1853), S.J. Williams (1859), A.S. Williams (1860-1864), S.T. Williams (1868), A.S. Williams (1872-1873), Charles Edwards Brewery Ltd (1914-1938).

THE BULL INN, NO. 12, ST JOHN'S SQUARE (ABERGAVENNY POST OFFICE)

The original three-storey, bay-windowed building dated back to the seventeenth century but was demolished to make way for the present post office in 1958. It is first recorded as a public house in 1787, with a Mr Williams as publican. In 1791, William Matthews is named as both publican and freeholder.

On Christmas Eve 1823, a Society of Tradesmen and Gentlemen was established at the pub and in March 1828 the Old Bull Friendly Society was also founded, with publican Hannah Williams as treasurer. The society was still going strong in 1836, when John Dunlop was the publican, but switched its allegiance to the King's Head in July 1837.

John Hurcum, the landlord between 1842 and 1844, also ran a brewery on the premises. In 1852, the publican, William Williams, was described as a 'victualler and carrier, licensed to let horses'.

Before the coming of the railway to Abergavenny in the mid-1850s, any goods not made locally had to be brought in on stage wagons drawn by huge teams of horses. In around 1880, 'an Abergavenny Octogenarian' recalled that:

> The stage waggons from London put up at the Bull Inn, in Nevill-street, and where the adjoining shops stand at the corner turning into Castle-street, were two large gates opening into a spacious yard. This yard at one time was the scene of most of the cock fights in Abergavenny, which, at one time, were not of unfrequent occurrence.

This yard and gate can be clearly seen on Wood's 1834 map of Abergavenny and is marked 'Carriers' Office'.

In 1897, the police opposed the renewal of the pub's licence on the grounds that 'there had been eight convictions recorded against the house, while the present tenant had been fined 20s and costs for being drunk on his licensed premises'. The owner, Mr Williams, wanted the new licence to be given to his son. The *Abergavenny Chronicle* for 27 August 1897 records that 'The Bench ... called Mr Williams and told him that they would give the Bull Inn another trial, and that his son must look after the business better in future'.

In his memoirs of old Abergavenny, Charles Price recalls a particularly dramatic incident at the pub in the 1920s:

> One holiday weekend when the town was full of miners and steel men, tremendous commotions were going on in St John's Square. My bedroom was on the top floor of No.16 [Nevill Street], but the row woke me up and I could see that the square and the bottom end of Nevill Street was teeming with people. Apparently the publican of The Bull had kicked out one of the miners and caused him some serious injury to his eye. Consequently all the miners in other pubs came along for revenge on the publican, Mr Edwards. I have a vivid memory of that night with hundreds of men yelling 'Crucify him, crucify him'. Edwards had taken care to barricade his door and windows. Those were the days!

The proprietor of the Bull Inn, James Weeks, in 1911.

The Bull Inn decorated for the Coronation of George V in 1911.

The Bull Inn in a sorry state, just prior to its demolition in 1957.

When the Bull Inn's licence as a public house was withdrawn in 1929, William Edwards, the publican, moved to the shop at No. 34, Nevill Street. He let rooms in the old pub until its demolition in 1958.

Publicans: Mr Williams (1787), William Matthews (1791), J. Williams (1822-1823), Hannah Williams (1828-1835), John Dunlop (1836), James Chamberlain (1839), John Hurcum (1842-1844), William Williams (1850-1884), William Morgan (1891), Lane Fowkes (1895), James Weeks (1901-1914), William Edwards (1923-1929).
Owners (when known): William Matthews (1791), William Morgan (1839), Mrs Hannah Williams (1850-1851), 'late Mrs Williams' (1853), William Williams (1859-1873), representatives of W.P. Williams (1914).

Other pubs recorded in St John's Square in the last century, but whose exact locations are not known, include:

THE SIX BELLS
This pub is first recorded as a beerhouse in 1850, under the management of William Tombs. It is first called the Six Bells in the Rate Book dated 30 May 1850. In 1852, William Tombs is described as a beer retailer and shopkeeper. By 1871, the house had been taken over by Thomas Monks. In 1873, he was still living in the same building but it is only listed in the Street and Water Rate Book as a house.

Publicans: William Tombs (1850-1865), Thomas Monks (1871-1873).
Owners (when known): 'late William Price' (1850-1853), W. James (1859), Mrs Prosser (1860), Mr James (1864), Mrs Prosser (1868-1873).

THE QUARRYMEN'S ARMS
This pub is first recorded in 1839, as a 'beershop' run by Mary Davies. It is only referred to as the Quarrymen's Arms in 1868, when it is recorded that the Street and Water rates could not be collected because the landlord, J. Churchill, had 'left the house'. The pub is not listed in the 1871 trade directory and had certainly closed by 1873.

Publicans: Mary Davies (1839-1853), James Davies (1858-1862), J. Jones (1864), John Morgan (1865), J. Churchill (1868).
Owners (when known): Samuel Phillips (1839), John Morgan (1850-1873).

TRINITY STREET

Only one beerhouse is recorded in Trinity Street, that of James Watkins in 1850. Its exact whereabouts are unknown.

TUDOR STREET

THE ALBION INN, NO. 1, TUDOR STREET
Built sometime after 1800, this pub is first recorded in the 1850 Poor Rate Book as a beerhouse run by Ann Powell. In 1859, the publican is recorded simply as 'Deleme'. This is probably the John Deleme

The former Albion Inn as it was in the mid-1950s.

listed in the 1858 trade directory as a beer retailer in Tudor Street. The pub is first called the Albion Inn in 1868, when it is described as vacant. It had certainly closed by 1873.

Publicans: Mrs Ann Powell (1850-1851), John Deleme (1858-1859), ? Williams (1860).
Owners (when known): John Rees (1850-1851), Captain Davies (1859-1860), C.B. Davies (1868).

THE TUDOR ARMS, NO. 8, TUDOR STREET
(formerly the Bush Inn)

Originally known as the Bush Inn, this pub stood at the top of Byfield Lane on the site directly opposite the present Tudor Gate surgery. It is first recorded in 1822. In March 1823, the house belonged to John Nicholas 'of Abergavenny, blacksmith' and Samuel Jones, farmer, of Llanspyddid, who leased it to William Nicholas 'of Abergavenny, wheelwright'. The earliest known publican is John Rees.

In 1852, the publican, James Chamberlain, is described as a 'victualler and shop-keeper'. By 1873, the pub was owned by Samuel Henry Facey as one of his tied houses (*see* Market Street). The pub was first called the Tudor Arms in 1895. It is last recorded as a pub in 1914 and the 1939 Rate Book describes it as a tenement.

Publicans: John Rees (1822), George Hill (1830-1835), William Nicholas (1839-1840), Henry Morgan (1842), William Chamberlain (1850), James Chamberlain (1851-1853), William Knight (1856), Thomas Price (1859-1868), Charles Halliburton (1872), Roderick Dallas (1873-1877; listed as Richard in 1873), Thomas Powell (1876), Joseph John Griffiths (1884), James Lewis Watkins (1891-1895), Lewis Morgan (1901-1906), Abraham Authers (1910-1912), William Manuel (1914).
Owners (when known): John Nicholas and Samuel Jones (March 1823), William Nicholas (March 1823-1840), Mrs Nicholas (1850), Mr Nicholas (1851), 'late Mr Nicholas' (1853), 'J. Ellis and Others'(1856-1864), ? Price (1868), James Price (1872), Samuel Henry Facey (1873), Frank Henry Facey (1914).

The former Tudor Arms is the large building on the left.

THE BLUE BELL INN, NO. 15, TUDOR STREET
(formerly the Bell Inn)

Originally known as the Bell Inn, this pub stood on the site now occupied by the Tudor Street police station and was demolished in 1957. The earliest record of the Bell Inn dates to 1822, when Nicholas Downing was the publican. In 1840, publican Nancy Price also ran a slaughterhouse on the site.

By 1894, the pub had become known as the Blue Bell. In 1897, the police opposed the renewal of the pub's licence on the grounds that 'the present tenant had been convicted twice during this year, and that he was not a fit and proper person to hold the licence.' The Bench renewed the licence but 'hoped the house would never come before them again'. At about the same time, an Abergavenny Octogenarian recorded a very interesting anecdote about one of the former publicans:

> The Pentre was built within my recollection for a Captain Frederick, of Crickhowell. I remember the plate being stolen. The thief was the proprietor of the Bell public house, in Tudor-street. He was found with the property in his possession, and was transported.

Frederick Fredericks was certainly living at the Pentre by 1819 and sold it in around 1845 to Mr Robert Wheeley, so any one of the publicans recorded between those dates could have been the culprit! It may be that the old local legend that the Tintern Treasure was buried under the pub is a memory of this real-life crime.

In his memoirs published in Abergavenny in the twentieth century, Charles Price recalled that:

> A Mr and Mrs Winter and family ran the pub ... [it] had a skittle alley at the rear of the house. The skittle balls were rolled back to base by means of stone slabs with a wide groove fixed in them atop a low wall.

The house is last recorded as a pub in 1914, with Edward Winter as landlord. In 1939, it is described as 'a house and garden' occupied by E. Winter and owned by a Mrs Weeks.

Above left and right: *The Blue Bell Inn shortly before demolition in 1957.*
Below: *Early seventeenth-century wall paintings discovered in the Blue Bell during its demolition in 1957.*

Publicans: Nicholas Downing (1822-1823), John Jayne (1830), David Price (1835), James Powell (1839), Nancy Price (1840), James Morgan (1842-1844), William Prosser (1850-1860), Henry Bath (1862), William Williams (1864-1865), William Hodges (1868-1877, also Joseph Adams in 1876), Job Davies (1880), Elijah Davies (1884), John Price (1891), William Bennett (1894-1895), John Buzzard (1901), Edward Henry Winter (1906-1914), E. Winter (1939).

Owners (when known): James Powell (1839), Nancy Price (1840), 'late John Davies' (1850-1853), Charles Davies (1859-1860), Mrs Wheeley (1864-1873), Arnold Perett & Co. Brewery Ltd (May 1914), James Weeks (June 1914), Mrs Weeks (1939).

THE TUDOR INN, NO. 22, TUDOR STREET
(formerly the Cymreigyddion Inn, the Volunteers Hall Inn and the Volunteer Inn)

Number 22, Tudor Street was a seventeenth-century building altered and embellished in the late eighteenth century. Between 1805 and 1829, the house was used as a meeting place by the Wesleyan Methodists. In 1844, a large hall was built at the back of the building by Edward Lewis for the Abergavenny Cymreigyddion Society, as a venue for their huge and internationally famous eisteddfodau.

The earliest reference to the use of No. 22 as a public house dates to 1850, when it was known as the Cymreigyddion Inn, under the management of Edward Lewis. For a brief period around 1862, it became known as the Volunteers Hall Inn due to the use of the hall by the Abergavenny Volunteer Rifle Company as a drill hall. By 1865, the pub had reverted to its original name but in 1873 it was again known as the Volunteer Inn. By 1875, the name had changed to the Tudor Inn. The hall was later used as a theatre and for public readings and finished its life as a boxing booth and gymnasium.

The Cymreigyddion Hall, later known as the Cymreigyddion Inn, the Volunteer Inn and the Tudor Inn. This picture was taken just before its demolition in 1957.

Publicans: Edward Lewis (1850-1860), Hannah Crates (1862-1865), 'Cook for Phillips' (1868), ? Gwatkin (1873), Charles Evans (1875-1877).
Owners (when known): Edward Lewis (1850-1868), Nathaniel Cook (1872), Edward Lewis (1873).

THE MILKMAN'S ARMS, NO. 40, TUDOR STREET
(formerly the Odd Fellows' Arms)
This is first recorded in 1850 as a beerhouse run by Joseph Robson. He had moved to Tudor Street from the Dog Inn on Ross Road. By 1852, his new house was known as the Odd Fellows' Arms. He had left the pub by July 1853. In 1860, the Street and Water Rate Book records that the rates could not be collected because the landlord, Samuel Brown, had 'Left the Country without paying'! By 1873, when the pub is last recorded, it was known as the Milkman's Arms.

Publicans: Joseph Robson (1850-1853), Samuel Brown (1856-1860), T. Nolan (1868), Thomas Gunter (1872-1873).
Owners (when known): Mr Elick (1853), James Elick (1856-1873).

THE OLD CROSS KEYS INN, NO. 41, TUDOR STREET
The Cross Keys stood on the site now occupied by the Benefits Office and Jobcentre building near the corner of Tudor Street and Baker Street. It is first listed in 1822. In 1852, two landlords are listed for the pub in the same directory, Ann Powell and John Bowcott. It had become known as the Old Cross Keys by 1868. Charles Price records fond memories of the place in his youth:

> And I must not forget Goff Morgan of the Cross Keys Inn on the corner of Baker Street and Tudor Street. He was very good rugby player who turned out for Newport and I think was also a trial player for the Welsh XV. His bar was festooned with pictures of famous boxers such as Jimmy Wild, Bombardier Wells and many others. I was fascinated.

The corner of Tudor Street and Baker Street shortly before demolition in 1957. On the left is the Old Cross Keys Inn.

Happier days – the Old Cross Keys decorated for the Coronation of Elizabeth II in 1953.

Publicans: John Powell (1822-1830), Thomas Pritchard (1835), Henry Morgan (1839-1840), Mrs Bowcott (May 1850), Ann Powell (1850), Mr Bowcott (1851), Ann Powell (1852), John Bowcott (1852-1853), T. Humphreys (1864), Mary Taylor (1868; 'William Lewis' crossed out), Theophilus Jones (1872), Thomas Adams (1873-1901; listed as 'Joseph Adams' in 1877), Mrs Jane Adams (1906), Richard Adams (1910-1912), Godfrey 'Goff' Morgan (1914-1926), listed but landlords not recorded (1927-1938), D.E. Thomas (1939).

Owners (when known): John Lewis (1839-1851), 'late John Lewis' (1853), A. Fairchild (1864), William Lewis (1868-1873), William Morgan Lewis (1880), Alton Court Brewery Co. (1914-1939).

THE COOPER'S ARMS, NO. 46, TUDOR STREET

The Cooper's Arms stood opposite the Old Cross Keys Inn on the southern side of Tudor Street. The first known publican is W. Price in 1822. This may be the 'William Price, Inn holder' who is recorded on the St Mary's churchyard survey as having died in 1825. The landlord in 1851 was Benjamin Whistance, who had previously kept the Gate House in Monk Street.

In February 1897, the pub was on lease to Arnold, Perrett & Co. Ltd of Wickwar Brewery but was advertised for sale by public auction at the Greyhound Hotel and described as:

> containing Smoke Room, Parlour, Fitted Bar, Kitchen, 4 Bedrooms, and Cellar, with Outbuildings at the rear … The attention of Brewers, Publicans and others is desired, as the house is situate in a good position in a very populous working-class neighbourhood.

However, by August the pub had still not been sold and the police opposed the renewal of the pub's licence on the grounds that 'there were five fully licensed, and two alehouses within 250 yards of the house'. The licence was refused and by 1901 the house was being run as a shop by Richard Dunden.

Publicans: W. Price (1822-1825?), William Tanner (1830), John Bowcott (1835-1850), P. Prosser (May 1850), Benjamin Whistance (1851), William Warr (1859-1865), Mrs Williams (1868), Thomas Denner (1871), ? Cox (1872), William Edwards (1873), Thomas Price (1875-1884), Mrs Maria Richards (1891), James Richards (1895).

The large building on the extreme left is No. 46, Tudor Street, the Cooper's Arms.

Owners (when known): Mrs Price (1839-June 1851), Elizabeth Price (July 1851-1856), Mrs Price (1859-1873).

THE FORESTER'S ARMS, NO. 67, TUDOR STREET

Prior to its demolition, the Forester's Arms stood on what is now the vacant lot on the corner of Pant Lane and Tudor Street. The earliest record of its use as a pub dates to 1850, when it was run as a beerhouse. It is first called the Forester's Arms in 1852. For forty-one years, from 1914 to 1955, the pub was run by the Davis family, first by Archibald Davis and then by his wife, Maud. Archibald's brother, Albin, ran the Old Duke Inn in Castle Street.

Publicans: George Pugh (1850-1852), John Price (1853-1865), John Denner (1868-1891), Thomas Richards (1895-1901), Herbert Vest (1906-1910), Archibald Davis (1914-1933), Maud M. Davis (1933-1955).
Owners (when known): Mrs Mary Lewis (1851-1853), John Lewis (1859), A. Yarworth (1860), Miss Bailey (1864), William Watkins (1868-1873), Brecon Brewery Co. (1914), Hereford and Tredegar Brewery (1938).

THE COCK AND BOTTLE, THE ROOKERY, PANT LANE

The Cock and Bottle occupied the ancient farmhouse formerly known as The Pant, which gave its name to Pant Lane and which certainly dated back as far as 1667. At the end of the nineteenth century, an Abergavenny Octogenarian recalled that in his boyhood 'the only house on the Grofield (or Grove Field) was Pant's house, now called the "Rookery"'.

The earliest reference to the house as pub dates to 1787, when a Mr Davies was the landlord. In August 1792, William Gough, victualler, and William Johnson, gentleman, leased the premises with other 'dwelling houses in Tyder otherwise Tuder Street' to Thomas Maddy of Hereford, currier. In October of the same year, William Gough leased it again, this time to William Powell of Abergavenny, victualler, for three years. The actual lease, dated 29 October, mentions 'the brewhouse, buildings, garden yard and skittle alley' – the earliest record of skittles being played in Abergavenny!

The Forester's Arms in the 1950s.

William Powell does not seem to have stayed for his full term because, in November 1793, William Gough leased the pub (yet again!) to William Warner of Abergavenny, maltster, who is listed as the publican of the King's Head from 1787 to 1791.

By 1830, the property had passed to Baker Gabb as part of the Grofield estate. The site is now occupied by a bungalow, which is still called The Rookery.

Publicans: Mr Davies (1787), William Davies (1791), William Maddy (August 1792-October 1792), William Powell (October 1792-November 1793), William Warner (November 1793).
Owners: William Gough and William Johnson (August 1792), William Gough (October 1792-November 1793).

THE BEAUFORT ARMS, NO. 96, TUDOR STREET

The Beaufort Arms in Tudor Street is only recorded twice, in 1839 and 1840. The owner of the property was John Lewis but the pub was run by Philip Price. By comparing the 1839 and 1840 Poor Rate Book entries and Wood's map of 1834, it is obvious that the pub stood at the entrance to Lewis's Yard at the western end of Westgate Buildings, in the house later known as No. 96, Tudor Street (opposite Westgate Cottage).

Publicans: Philip Price (1839-1840).
Owners (when known): John Lewis (1839-1840).

Other pubs listed in Tudor Street but whose exact locations are not known, include:

THE HORSE SHOE

Mr Samuel (1787), William Samuel (1791).

THE ROSE AND CROWN

Mrs Thomas (1787), William Adams (1791).

THE GLAMORGAN INN

The Glamorgan Inn stood somewhere near the Bush Inn, possibly in Byfield Lane. It is only recorded once, in 1859.

Publicans: Henry Bleakmore (1859).
Owners (when known): W. Morgan (1859).

BEERHOUSES

NO. 26, TUDOR STREET

This building was built in the period 1590-1610. Inside, it had oak stud and panel partition walls, stone flag floors and an upper cruck roof. Parts of the house were decorated with sixteenth- or seventeenth-century wall paintings. The premises are recorded as a beerhouse for a brief period between 1868 and 1873.

Publicans: David Williams (1868), E. White (1873).
Owners (when known): Trustees of the Independent Chapel (1868-1873).

Other beer retailers, exact whereabouts unknown, include:
William Price (1835), John Smith (1835), Thomas Delafield (1862), James James (1862), Thomas Richards (1862), William Morgan (1862), William Hodges (1865; by 1868 he was the publican of the Blue Bell Inn), Francis Humfries (1865), James Carter (1871), William Ross (1871).

JAMES GOUGH'S BREWERY, BEHIND NO. 35, TUDOR STREET

The large building that stood behind No. 35, Tudor Street, facing onto Baker Street, served as a malthouse under various owners from at least 1839. However, between 1873 and 1877 it is recorded as a brewery owned by James Gough. By 1884, he had moved to the Royal Victoria Brewery further along Baker Street (see above) and had also bought the Old Fountain Inn in Frogmore Street. He sold both in 1888.

No. 26, Tudor Street in 1957.

Tudor Street during the demolitions of 1957. The large building by the tree is Gough's Brewery.

UNION ROAD

NO. 55, UNION ROAD
The first reference to a beer-retailing business at this address dates to 1884, when it was run by Daniel Delafield, whose father ran Delafield's Brewery at the King's Arms in Nevill Street. In June 1903, he became the licensee of the Sun Inn, and the Union Road business was transferred to Ada Delafield.

Publicans: Daniel Delafield (1884-1903), Miss Ada Cornelia Mary Delafield (1903-1914), William George Champ (1923), Mrs Rose Champ (1926), William Samuel Webb (1934-1937), Ivor J. Taylor (1938-15 November 1938), ? Watkins (15 November 1938-1939)
Owners (when known): representatives of Thomas Delafield (1914), Arnold Perret & Co. Brewers (1938).

VICTORIA STREET
Victoria Street is first referred to as such in the 1851 Rate Book. Prior to that, it was known as Grofield High Street or treated as part of Frogmore Street.

THE BEAUFORT ARMS, NO. 26, VICTORIA STREET
This pub started out as a beerhouse and is first recorded in June 1851, with John Jenkins as publican. It was first called the Beaufort Arms in 1852, when the address was listed as 'High Street, Grofield'. The Beaufort Arms was the last pub in Abergavenny to brew its own beer. Mr Charles Henry Rolfe took over the premises in 1923 and continued brewing there until 1946.

Publicans: John Jenkins (June 1851-1853), William Burnell (1862-1877), Mrs Ann Burnell (1884), Samuel Roberts (1891), John M. Denner (1895-1914), William Williams (1923), Charles Henry Rolfe (1923-1946).
Owners (when known): John Jenkins (July 1851), Mary Price (1853), M.A. Price (1864-1873), John M. Denner (1914), Charles Henry Rolfe (1938).

The Beaufort Arms, c.1930, with the proprietors Charles and Helen Rolfe, their daughter Ada and Buster the spaniel.

THE MOUNT PLEASANT INN, NO. 53, VICTORIA STREET

This building is first recorded as a shop run by James Curtis in June 1851. The earliest mention of it as a pub dates to 1862, when Thomas Curtis is listed as a 'beer retailer and potato dealer'. By 1871, the business was being run by his wife, Ann. In 1894, David Curtis of Brynmawr mortgaged the pub to Anette Williams, also of Brynmawr, for the sum of £120. This is the first record of the pub by the name of the Mount Pleasant.

In September 1896, the pub was sold to Charles Garton and Co. Brewers of Bristol. By 1906, the pub was owned by the Anglo-Bavarian Brewery of Shepton Mallet and in November of that year they leased the house to George Benjamin Beavan. By 1938, it was owned by Perret and Co. of Bristol.

Publicans: Thomas Curtis (1862-1865), Mrs Griffiths (1868), Mrs Ann Curtis (1871-1873), Walter Jones (1875-1884), William Chamberlain (1891), David Curtis (1895), George B. Beavan (1906-1914), Tom Edwards (1923-1926), Thomas Parsons (1934-1939).
Owners (when known): Thomas Curtis (1864), Mr Curtis (1868), Mrs Ann Curtis (1873), David Curtis (1894), Charles Garton and Co. (1896), Anglo-Bavarian Brewery (1906), Garton & Co. (1914), Arnold Perret & Co. Brewers (1938).

BEERHOUSES

Other beer retailers recorded in Victoria Street but whose whereabouts are unknown, include Henry Bowen (1842-1844) and John Morgan (1850).

The Mount Pleasant sometime between 1906 and 1914.

Endnote

Since the 1590s, public houses have both reflected and contributed to the unique character of Abergavenny. In the days before civic amenities, they acted as eating houses, banks, magistrates courts, council chambers, theatres, concert halls and cultural venues. They hosted plays, boxing, bull-baiting, militia drills, Bible classes, political and literary meetings and (almost incidentally) eating, drinking and unruly behaviour!

The very names of the pubs themselves are a roll-call of the social history of the town. The loyalty of 'Catholic Burgavenny' to the house of Stuart was represented by the King's Arms and Jacobite Raven. On the other side of the religious and political divide, the White Horse signified the acceptance by some at least of Abergavenny's citizens of Protestant Hanoverian rule. The Earl Grey and the Two Reformers are redolent of the growth of radical politics and the campaign for electoral reform in the nineteenth century.

The Sun was one of the badges of the house of York during the Wars of the Roses. Abergavenny's importance as a stronghold of Yorkist sympathy was memorialised not just by the now long-lost pub name, but also by the magnificent tombs of Yorkist nobles in St Mary's priory church. The Sun also claims its place in the history of Welsh culture as the birthplace of the largest Welsh cultural movement of the nineteenth century. It could stake a legitimate claim to being the birthplace of the National Eisteddfod as we know it. Is it not time to restore this historic name to the house that bore it for so long?

A study of the history of a town's pubs is, almost inevitably, a study of its social history, its character and its sense of place. Abergavenny is no exception and long may it continue!

Index